# Religious Sociology

Recent Titles in Contributions in Sociology
*Series Editor: Don Martindale*

Social Cohesion: Essays Toward a Sociophysiological Perspective
*Patricia R. Barchas and Sally P. Mendoza, editors*

Family and Work: Comparative Convergences
*Merlin B. Brinkerhoff, editor*

No Place to Hide: Crisis and Future of American Habitats
*Manuel Marti, Jr.*

Systems of Discourse: Structures and Semiotics in the Social Sciences
*George V. Zito*

Ideologies, Goals, and Values
*Feliks Gross*

People's Poland: Patterns of Social Inequality and Conflict
*Wladyslaw Majkowski*

Weeding Out the Target Population: The Law of Accountability in a
Manpower Program
*James Latimore*

Social Responses to Technological Change
*Augustine Brannigan and Sheldon Goldenberg, editors*

Overload and Boredom: Essays on the Quality of Life in the
Information Society
*Orrin E. Klapp*

Charisma, History, and Social Structure
*Ronald M. Glassman and William H. Swatos, Jr., editors*

The Underside of High-Tech: Technology and the Deformation of
Human Sensibilities
*John W. Morphy, Algis Mickunas, and Joseph J. Pilotta, editors*

Five Scenarios for the Year 2000
*Franco Ferrarotti*

Uniforms and Nonuniforms: Communication Through Clothing
*Nathan Joseph*

Housing Markets and Policies under Fiscal Austerity
*Willem van Vliet—, editor*

# RELIGIOUS SOCIOLOGY
## INTERFACES AND BOUNDARIES

EDITED BY

## William H. Swatos, Jr.

CONTRIBUTIONS IN SOCIOLOGY, NUMBER 64

Greenwood Press
NEW YORK • WESTPORT, CONNECTICUT • LONDON

For Priscilla, Giles, and Eric _____

Library of Congress Cataloging-in-Publication Data
Religious sociology.
  (Contributions in sociology, ISSN 0084-9278 ; no. 64)
  Bibliography: p.
  Includes index.
  1. Religion and sociology.   I. Swatos, William H.
II. Series.
BL60.R45   1987        306'.6        87-353
ISBN 0-313-25528-8 (lib. bdg. : alk. paper)

Library of Congress Catalog Card Number: 87-353
ISBN: 0-313-25528-8
ISSN: 0084-9278
First published in 1987
Greenwood Press, Inc.
88 Post Road West, Westport, Connecticut 06881
Printed in the United States of America

The paper used in this book complies with the
Permanent Paper Standard issued by the National
Information Standards Organization (Z39.48-1984).
10  9  8  7  6  5  4  3  2  1

Copyright Acknowledgments
Grateful acknowledgment is rendered to the following:
The Association for the Sociology of Religion, for permission to reprint Benton Johnson's essay, as an abridgmentof his article "Socio-
logical Theory and Religious Truth," which appeared in the official
journal of the Association, *Sociological Analysis*, 1977 38(4): 368–
88.
L. Shannon Jung for permission to use his article on the theology of
story from *Religion In Life*, Autumn, 1977. Copyright © 1977 by
Abingdon Press.
Irving Louis Horowitz for granting permission to George A. Hillery,
Jr., to contribute his revision of "Freedom, Love, and Community,"
which appeared in *transaction/SOCIETY*, May/June 1978, 24--31.
Copyright © 1978 by Transaction, Inc.
The Religious Research Association for permission to reprint an ed-
ited version of William H. Swatos, Jr., "The Power of Prayer: A
Prolegomenon to an Ascetical Sociology," which appeared in the
*Review of Religious Research*, 1982, 24(2): 153–63.

# Contents

PREFACE                                                    vii

PART I.    ISSUES AND INTERFACES

    1.    Faith, Facts, and Values in the Sociology          3
          of Religion
          *Benton Johnson*

    2.    Sociology, Christianity, and Humanity             15
          *Jack O. Balswick*

PART II.   THEOLOGY AND SOCIOLOGY

    3.    Theology Lessons for Sociology                    27
          *Ronald J. McAllister*

    4.    The Sociological Theology of H. Richard           41
          Niebuhr
          *William R. Garrett*

    5.    A Sociological and Fraternal Perspective          57
          on James M. Gustafson's Ethics
          *Paul M. Gustafson*

    6.    Ethics and the Image of the Self in the           69
          Theology of Story
          *L. Shannon Jung*

**PART III. THE SOCIOLOGY OF FAITH**

7. On Freedom, Love, and Community       87
   *George A. Hillery, Jr.*

8. The Power of Prayer: Observations and       103
   Possibilities
   *William H. Swatos, Jr.*

9. The Invisible Religion of Catholic       115
   Charismatics
   *Pierre Hegy*

10. Militant Religion       125
    *Eugen Schoenfeld*

**PART IV. APPLYING RELIGIOUS SOCIOLOGY**

11. The Psychological Captivity of       141
    Evangelicalism
    *Jack O. Balswick*

12. Clinical Pastoral Sociology       153
    *William H. Swatos, Jr.*

NOTES       165

BIBLIOGRAPHY       177

INDEX       189

ABOUT THE CONTRIBUTORS       193

# Preface

This book began its course to production slightly over a decade ago when some grant moneys enabled me to organize a lecture series entitled "Sociology and Christian Believing" at the college where I was then teaching. At that time the "interface" of sociology and religion was not particularly a scene for *aggiornamento*. The secularization thesis was still quite popular in the sociology of religion. Marxism had undermined functionalist hegemony in general theory. And an increasing turn toward the religious right suggested that religionists might have had their fill of sociological analyses. Strangely, all of this proved at once true and false. Today we have explicit books on the relationship of sociology and Christianity,[1] some evangelical condemnations of fellow-evangelical sociologists,[2] Marxist Christianity and Christian Marxism,[3] and so on. The secularization thesis, though by no means abandoned, has undergone radical revision. Religion has proved far more malleable than not only its critics, but also some of its mourning friends, had imagined.[4]

In all of this, however, there remains a void in enabling a forum for an interactive discussion of critical issues between sociology and religion. This book seeks to address this specific problematic. Its purpose is to make clear how complex the sociology-religion interface really is and how much further we have to go before we achieve a modicum of success.

St. Thomas Aquinas sought to demonstrate that God could be known not only through revelation but also through reason, experience, and observation. His five "proofs" for the existence of God, often sadly caricatured both by those who wish to advance the cause of Christian religion and by those who oppose it, were an attempt to say that the world of revelation and the world of human experience are not two worlds but one. The universe mirrors its Creator. Revelation takes place within the universe by virtue of the persons, places, and things that exist in it. Thus, there ought not to be an opposition between the world of science and the world of religion. For Aquinas, theology was science, the queen of the sciences, the science of God. It was an attempt to understand God through a total revelation of divine being in and through the created universe. Norman Birnbaum says in much the same vein—although certainly not because of any Thomistic convictions—that theology should be "not an immutable doctrine, but a science describing the interpenetration of the spiritual and the concrete."[5]

Modern "creationism" notwithstanding, the so-called religion and science "debate" has been resolved to a considerable degree in relation to the natural and physical sciences.[6] But it is not at all clear that the tension of this false opposition has been adequately resolved for social science in general or sociology in particular. This book will not resolve this tension either. To the contrary, it will be most successful to the extent that it raises questions rather than answers them, to the degree that it challenges rather than comforts, provokes rather than soothes. Age-old tensions remain: love and justice, cognition and emotion, transcendence and immanence. What these essays show, however, is that these are not merely philosophical postures, but real action systems with sociological consequences for human beings in this world. How they are resolved makes a difference to how we think and live.

There are, however, uniting themes within the book. The first is conceptualized in the phrase *religious sociology*, by which I mean not the gathering of data for ecclesiastical purposes—as the phrase is sometimes used (especially in European contexts)—but rather "sociology as if religion is real." All of these essays are characterized by a core principle of *non-reductionism*. This is a framework that I have elsewhere described as a situational approach.[7] This is not to say that each of the authors has "bought into" situationalism as a specific definitional framework; rather, the essays as collected illustrate the value of a situational perspective.

There is a strain in the sociology of American sociology that likes to engage from time to time in a friendly masochism of sorts. "Why aren't we better than we are?" One of the answers that often pops up is a supposed history of religious "interests" in American sociology that distinguishes it from European sociology.[8] This is a grossly distorted rendering of the history of sociology on both sides of the Atlantic. Yes, religious interests did propel some early American sociologists, but so did anti-religious interests. European sociologists, furthermore, clearly had religious "interests"—pro or con—from Comte on. Who of the European "masters" did not take on religion in one form or another: Durkheim? Marx? Weber? Simmel? Spencer?[9] Indeed, the pejorative use of the phrase "religious sociology" to mean statistics-gathering to advance the cause of the church—better, I think, termed "ecclesiastic sociology"[10]— is European in origin.

A second theme throughout the essays is *faith*, the conscious acknowledgment that there is no presuppositionless action and certainly no presuppositionless science. All human life depends upon trust or faith, upon statements "taken-for-true," an important criterion for which is experience. Differences in experiences lead us to accept different criteria for "truth," and as George Hillery points out, different types of "truth" in different settings. The wonderfully liberating observation that Peter Berger makes in *A Rumor of Angels* that the ultimate consequence of sociology is that the relativizers are relativized is realized here.[11] We recognize that all truth is "true" from a perspective, and the weight of the arguments here, certainly, is for explicitness and integrity in making our perspectives clear— "coming out of the closet," as Benton Johnson puts it.

Sociology for most of its life has been multiparadigmatic. In all likelihood it is destined to remain so. The intent of this book, as Bill Garrett points out, is *not* to establish a "new Christian Sociology" (or, worse yet, revive the old), but to raise the consciousness of sociologists and religionists to the religious dimensions within sociology—the "faith commitments" of theoretical perspectives and their consequences—and the sociological dimensions within religion. In the latter case, we don't mean merely those well-worn grounds of organizational dynamics, "human relations," or even "material interests"; rather, that religion is at its very core a social experience—that to say "God is personal" is already to say something about the society in which one lives.[12]

This, then, leads to a third theme: *personalism*—speaking honestly from where we are about the world around us. As sociologists we are given to see things in certain ways and to use specific linguistic forms to describe and explain what we see; yet these are papers about what *we* see. Though some essays speak of it more explicitly than others, the entire book is an exercise in "story." Our discourse may not be *im*passioned, but it is not *dis*passionate either. The essays attempt to bring together experience and analysis in the best sociological tradition.

To make these assertions is neither to deify sociological theory nor to deny divine existence, revelation, or intervention. It is to speak about processes of human experience. It is at this very juncture that sociology and religion meet. Whether they merge or collide—interface or meet sharp boundaries—depends upon many things, some touched upon here and some not. We cannot guarantee a merger—some of us may not even be sure we would want to. Nor can we prevent a collision. This book will have made its contribution, however, if regardless of which happens, the participants in the action systems have a little better understanding of why.

The first two chapters, by Benton Johnson and Jack Balswick, form an introductory couplet, addressing each side of the religion-sociology coin. Johnson provides a historical analysis of how a supposed "detente" between sociology and religion was created in American sociology, largely at the hands of Talcott Parsons. Johnson also argues that the ground upon which this bargain was struck is hardly firm, and the current result is a gradual, but fairly clear, breaking apart of the deal. Religionists want more of a "piece" of sociology, and sociologists want to move on to religious truth questions. Balswick addresses the all-important topic of how "human being" is conceived in sociology vis-à-vis a biblical model. Not surprisingly, he finds that sociological theories tend to omit one or another central component. Some sociologies come far closer than others, however, and he thus raises the tantalizing question of why some sociologies are more popular than others. His point is not to conduct a biblical inquisition of sociology but rather to indicate that precisely as the era of detente is in decline it is important to clarify the boundaries in order to test the legitimacy of particular interfaces.

The second section of the book deals with the interface of theology and sociology. Ronald McAllister does something of a turn-about on contemporary trends—in which bits and pieces of sociology are being imported into theology—and suggests that sociology can learn something from theology. His argument goes in two directions: On the one hand, sociologists have had a naïve and negative view of theology; namely, that being a theologian meant being a dogmatic person or a dogmatist. There are undoubtedly dogmatic persons ("authoritarian personality" types) who will use the "findings" of theologians dogmatically to assert power over others, but this is not the function of theology. On the other hand, sociologists have been naïve about their own work, thinking it possible under the rubric of "value free" science to be "innocent" bystanders. McAllister reaffirms the principle that there are no "innocent" bystanders, that everyone confronted by an issue is involved morally in that issue, and that moral involvement involves ultimate commitments, regardless of whether they are or are not explicitly articulated. McAllister urges that since this is the case, we are all better off if we lay our moral cards on the table and state our positions as best we see them. Having to say where we stand forces us to confront the cogency of our positions.

The articles by William R. Garrett and Paul Gustafson in this section both are case studies of theologians. Garrett takes the "classic" figure of H. Richard Niebuhr and demonstrates through a careful textual analysis the influence upon him of George Herbert Mead. That Niebuhr was influenced by Mead is not a new finding in itself, since Niebuhr himself acknowledges Mead's work in later books. What *is* significant in Garrett's argument is that he dates Mead's influence to a far earlier period in Niebuhr's work and connects Mead's thought to Niebuhr's concepts of God and revelation, not merely to human relationships. Interestingly, Garrett ends his piece by noting that James Gustafson is one of the few theologians who has attempted to take the challenge of Niebuhr's rigorous intellectual demands in theology seriously. Paul Gustafson, then, begins his analysis of his brother's theology using the tools of sociological theory—particularly Wolfgang Schluchter's approach to Max Weber. In something close to a *tour de force*, Paul combines the richness of a whole life lived in awareness of his brother's work with a carefully structured, systematic theoretical analysis in sociology.

In the last essay of this section, L. Shannon Jung assesses the "theology of story" for both its sociological and theological adequacy. The theology of story is important because it is so consciously rooted in human experience. *Story* recognizes the importance of language and communication to the construction of "reality" as we know it. The theology of story is fundamentally sociological, rightly construed, yet at the same time promises to be able to read something of divinity out of the social experience as it is recounted. It furthermore argues that divinity is known to humanity only as the "word" is passed, the story is told.

Here we come full-circle: The role of theology is to express the essence of what it is that human beings as inherently social beings are saying to their fellows and to their God about their God (who is God in relationship)[13] and their lives before God. Theology gets into trouble when it begins to consider "God talk" outside of this *empirical*, experiential context. This is not in any sense to deny the importance of history in doing theology, but an insistence that history be taken as providing a human context to be treated as a whole (i.e., a culture) for analysis. Thus, "explanations come to an end somewhere,"[14] and if "God will be God," as James Gustafson asserts, then we had better recognize that it is both blasphemous and idolatrous to claim that the task of theology is either to justify or explain divinity. If a word play be permitted, sociology can remind theology that *to explain* in causal modeling is to explain *away*. God, who is incomprehensible,[15] needs no justification. The task of theology is to articulate the *experience* of God. What experience is that? A social experience.

The third section of the book explores the relevance of "religious sociology" for sociology in general, particularly as it manifests itself in the transition from theory to research. The article by George Hillery, first conceived for presentation in the lecture series from which this volume takes its origin,[16] has appeared previously in several places. It presents a discussion of his data on a variety of organizations, the most fascinating of which is monasteries. The paper has a larger significance, however, inasmuch as it illuminates the essential flaw of reductionist sociology: Not only is religion "reduced" away, but also such important areas of human life as freedom and love. Hillery at once presents creative measures that address these topics while at the same time pointing to the boundaries where some kind of knowing other than science must come into use.

In my essay on prayer, I raise the question of why there has been so little sociological investigation of prayer when so many people do it. I suggest that the sociology of religion has paid too much attention to external organizational variables and preconceived theological images and too little to what people actually do and say when they are being religious. Though he is not entirely happy with my emphasis on the power variable, Pierre Hegy takes my general thrust one step further by observing charismatic Christians without attempting to apply sociological categories. To the contrary, he uses his participant observation data on these people to test a variety of sociological concepts and theories and finds them wanting. He suggests, in effect, that we reconstruct the sociology of religion from the religion of people who are religious. This is the approach that I have termed situationalism.[17] The final essay of this section by Eugen Schoenfeld also reflects this orientation. In particular, Schoenfeld wants to ask why and how it is that in fact religious people are sometimes militant, rather than the "yea-sayers" that some sociological theories—notably vulgar Marxism—claim they are. From the civil rights movement to the new right, from Jerusalem to Teheran, from Maccabeus to Paisley, religious people have said "no" to political authority. What are the situations that call forth militancy? Why does some militancy reach out while other forms cut off?

In the final section of the book, Jack Balswick and I are concerned with applied issues. We both are interested in the peculiar lack of a sociological consciousness on the part of religious practitioners. Jack focuses more on evangelicals; I, more on liberals. Our points, however, are essentially the same: Religious people have largely embraced and canonized psychology as if it were sent from heaven. Pastoral counseling, pastoral psychology, clinical pastoral education are dominated by psychologism. When sociology is considered it is almost always in the guise of "social action"—viewed generally negatively by the evangelicals, positively by liberals. Sociological insights about the essential processes of human being are almost entirely neglected. The result is a very weak understanding of the person and of persons-in-relationship. We do not, of course, reject the insights of psychology, but we suggest that sociological models of human being offer a more complete understanding of the human condition than is now generally received and at the same time provide the basis to critique specific assumptions—e.g., the medical model—inherent in psychologism. Sociological models in the context of religious sociology as conceived here provide a setting for taking religion seriously that psychologism lacks. The conclusion to my essay is also intended to be a conclusion to the book. The point of this section is that if what we have collectively discussed through the bulk of the volume cannot be applied, it is of little value.

In addition to the publishers who gave us permissions along the way, I owe some specific debts to people who were willing to commit themselves to this project at one stage or another: Larry Hitner, who got the money for the lecture series with which it began; Bill Ramsay, who sat through all the lectures and wrote an introduction to a book that never was; and Sherri Alexander, who typed that aborted draft. Ron Glassman gave me the motivation to try again and listened to me whine all through the editorial process. The authors of the essays have each drafted, redrafted, and suffered the pains of amputative surgery. I was sustained especially by George Hillery who never gave up the hope that this volume would be published and in fact talked about it in his own sociological autobiography, *A Research Odyssey*. The final editing and preparation of the manuscript for publication took place while I was supported by a grant from the World Society Foundation of Zürich, Switzerland. I am also grateful to several persons who contributed to the series or to earlier versions of this book whose work has not ultimately appeared in this collection and must await another time and place.

For some time I have credited St. Ignatius Loyola with the saying, "Pray as though everything depends upon God; work as though everything depends on you." Each of us has brought different amounts of these abilities to the book, but I am sure that it is here because of both.

# Part I. ISSUES AND INTERFACES

# 1. Faith, Facts, and Values in the Sociology of Religion

## Benton Johnson

Robert W. Friedrichs has spoken of the past two or three generations as a time of detente between social science and religion.[1] Although he has little to say about the contributions sociologists made to this state, it seems clear that two of their claims were essential to bringing it about. The first was the assertion that empirical science can say nothing definitive about the truth or falsity of religious beliefs. The second was the assertion that science is incompetent to make value judgments concerning religious practices and their effects. These two assertions formed the basis for a non-antagonistic division of labor between social scientists on the one hand and religionists on the other. The latter were to have sole jurisdiction over theological and moral judgments. The former claimed to be able to make only non-evaluative explanations of religious behavior.

Friedrichs has also observed that this detente is now in jeopardy. He has pointed to a few trends in sociology and related fields that have helped put it in jeopardy, but he has not seen that the intellectual basis for the accommodation between sociology and religion has been shaky from the very beginning. From varying perspectives and with varying degrees of clarity, an increasing number of sociologists are realizing just how shaky it is.[2] Their reactions to this insight have already begun to shatter the consensus that existed for so long in the field at the level of general theory. With the benefit of hindsight it is now possible to give a concise account of the intellectual problems to which these sociologists are responding.

First, there is a contradiction between the claim that sociology of religion is value neutral and the fact that contemporary sociological theories of religion do contain value judgments. Second, there is a contradiction between the claim that science can say nothing about religious truth and the fact that our theories do say something about it. At the level of general theory, sociology of religion implicitly endorses religion—or some aspects of it. On the question of religious truth, however, general theory is implicitly atheistic. Theory in our field has constrained sociologists to say, in effect, that although religious ideas are not true, much in religion is good.

Once this is perceived, a new contradiction appears. It is hard to endorse a way of life while believing there are no reasons for doing so. If one claims that some religion is true, there is substantial warrant for commending it to oneself and others. If one claims it is false, that warrant disappears. One must then find a new justification for the way of life once supported by religious faith or embrace an entirely new way that seems based on sound reasons. On the other hand, if one's heart remains with religion, one must find a defensible way of reaffirming the truth of its ideas. Sociologists can no longer keep their personal position on religion in the closet while they appear publicly in the neutral uniform of disciplinary professionalism. To put things in this way can help identify the problems that many sociologists of religion are now grappling with, as well as the directions in which their attempted solutions are taking them. It can also help us understand why many of them have begun taking sides in disputes formerly thought to be "off limits" in scientific discourse. As they have perceived various facets of these contradictions, many sociologists have begun coming out of religious closets.

## LOOKING BACKWARDS

Modern sociology of religion did not develop in a vacuum. It stands in sharp opposition to a set of theories of a very different sort. Although these theories have long been discredited, at least among American sociologists of religion, a brief review of their basic thrust will help explain how the foundations of our current perspective on religion came to be laid down. These earlier theories reflected the influence of the Enlightenment, with its high opinion of the role of reason in human affairs, its commitment to improving the general condition of humanity, and its belief that science is a superior method for discovering truth. The theories in question were as varied in specific content as the theories of Auguste Comte, Herbert Spencer, and Karl Marx. But at the core of all of them were two indictments of religion—or more specifically Christianity—in the name of human reason and well-being. The first indictment was the charge that religious teachings are not true; the second indictment was that religion has encouraged many practices that are inimical to human welfare. The basic message of this theoretical tradition, then, is that religion is neither good nor true by the standards of an enlightened age. The practical implication of these indictments was obvious: The sooner our historic religions are done away, the better.

Contemporary sociological theory responds to these indictments, on the other hand, by declaring on methodological grounds that they are inadmissible as scientific propositions. To the charge that religious practice is detrimental to human welfare, modern theory replies by invoking the doctrine that the methods of science provide no way of making value judgments. Science must be value free. To the charge that religious ideas are false, modern theory replies that religious ideas refer ultimately to a realm of reality that is non-empirical and therefore beyond the reach of scientific investigation. Modern theory laid the formal groundwork for the detente between religion and social science by dismissing as unscientific the indictments of earlier theories.

Talcott Parsons was the most influential architect of detente. It is difficult to overestimate his contribution to shaping modern sociological thinking about religion. Among other things, he helped introduce the works of Durkheim and Weber to American sociologists of religion.[3] But equally important, he made two judgments that rendered their works far more serviceable to the cause of religion than they might otherwise have been. First, he endorsed Weber's argument that social science must be value free,[4] rather than Durkheim's very different position on the role of values in science.[5] Second, he rejected Durkheim's view concerning the referent of religious symbols and replaced it with a proposition of his own. Whereas Weber had simply avoided the question of what religious ideas represent, Durkheim had insisted that they ultimately represent society itself. As an alternative, Parsons advanced the now widely accepted view that insofar as religious symbols assume the form of existential propositions they refer to "aspects of 'reality' ...outside the range of scientific investigation and analysis."[6]

## ON VALUE NEUTRALITY

The doctrine that scientific work must be value free is too well known to need reviewing in detail. Suffice it to say that the doctrine rests on the assumption that the aim of science is to achieve a true, i.e., factually correct, understanding of various aspects of the "real world." It declares that the language of science must be phrased in the indicative mood of the verb and that it must avoid expressing the investigator's wishes or feelings about the object of inquiry. Words like "ought" or "should" and any terms that are "emotive" must be excluded from scientific discourse. Such language must be excluded because it has the logical status of a command. Since commands are imperative rather than indicative, they have no truth value. That commands are neither true nor false can be demonstrated by considering what might be an appropriate response to the command, "Close the window." One might respond by asking "Why?," or by saying, "Do it yourself"; but it would be meaningless to respond by asking, "Is it true?"[7]

Certain Marxists, humanists, Christians, and others opposed to "positivistic" social science have always had reservations about the doctrine of value neutrality, and they have been especially suspicious of modern sociology's claim to be value free. In recent years some of them have tried to show that sociology contains many ideological elements.[8] Despite the fact that some of their revelations have been convincing, they have not resolved the complex issues which any serious critique of the doctrine of value neutrality would have to consider. It is possible, however, to make a clear distinction between the rational core of the doctrine and the various indefensible implications often drawn from it. Its rational core is the safeguard it provides against making erroneous judgments of fact concerning aspects of reality about which one wishes to know the truth. By making a strict distinction between what is and what we might wish to be the case, it protects the general interest in arriving at truth from contamination by our particular hopes or fears. It alerts us to the fact that we do not use the same methods to "test" a norm or a command as we use to test a hypothesis. It therefore reminds us that statements laying claim to truth cannot contain elements that are grammatically normative.

The rule of value neutrality cannot, however, purge scientific work of all value relevance. Even its strongest advocates acknowledge that values enter into the selection of scientific problems. Max Weber insisted on this point. Parsons, too, insists that scientific work itself is value relevant, in the sense that science must be legitimated in terms of commonly held values.[9] But advocates of value neutrality have seldom faced the fact that normative judgments about the objects of scientific inquiry are often built into scientific language itself. Long ago Gunnar Myrdal demonstrated that the very concepts sociologists use, e.g., the concept of social disorganization, tend to have evaluative connotations.[10] But Myrdal's observations were not widely discussed, perhaps because sociologists believed they could make their language value free by taking greater pains to avoid terms having evaluative overtones. It is now possible, however, to state quite emphatically that *there is no way to guarantee that social scientific language can be made value free.* The use of indicative verbs and the avoidance of emotive terms do not prevent sociologists from building theory that resonates with their value preferences. This can be demonstrated, again, by reflecting on the fact that in everyday life we often use indicative language to communicate wishes and commands. Instead of saying, "Close the window," which is grammatically imperative, we may say, "We're going to catch a cold if we leave the window open." This latter way of making our wishes felt is grammatically indicative. In fact, it is a testable hypothesis. But in the context in which it is likely to be used, everyone will understand that it is an indirect way to express a wish or command. Everyone will understand it that way because everyone will agree that it is undesirable to have a cold. The phrase "catch a cold" carries normative freight just as much as the term "social disorganization" does. But to purge sociological language of all value-laden terms would be to make the discipline irrelevant to anything most people care about. The alternative to addressing meaningful issues is to retreat into triviality. Religion is not a trivial matter to many people, while trivialization of religion is itself a religious stance.

## EVALUATIVE ELEMENTS IN THE SOCIOLOGY OF RELIGION

Once it is understood that a totally value free social scientific theory of religion cannot be constructed, it is possible to perceive that contemporary theory is on the whole quite favorable to religion. First, Parsons's very act of invoking the two methodological principles mentioned above was a friendly gesture. It helped lay the groundwork for the long period of detente between religion and social science by dismissing the old indictments of religion. Second, the basic substantive propositions of modern theory carry the clear implication that religion is a good thing. Modern theory tells us that religion provides meaningful and hopeful answers to the disappointments and catastrophes everyone faces at some time or other, that it supplies the ultimate legitimation for the core of common values that is essential to any coherent group life, and that it helps set the course of social change and personal development. These are *not* morally neutral propositions. They constitute the endorsement of religion that is concealed by the doctrine that neither indictments nor endorsements are scientifically permissible. Thus Gouldner, for example, has claimed that "there is no single institution to which Parsons attributes such potency and goodness" as the Christian church, which Parsons believes "has been the rock and the light of modern civilization."[11] Third, the curious fact that the modern theory of religion has been immune to serious testing suggests that many of its advocates dimly sense its role in legitimating religion and are not eager to face the prospect that it might be disconfirmed. Most of the middle-range theorizing and empirical research done by sociologists of religion (e.g., church-sect, 5-D) has little direct connection with general theory. Thus, the principal role of general theory seems to be to legitimate the study of religion and to provide a few general orientations to research (e.g., an aversion to Marxist analyses or the disposition to treat religion as an independent variable at certain points).

Finally, despite their dedication to a value free social science, the framers of modern theory themselves have occasionally made statements about religion that leave little doubt where their sympathies lie. It is revealing to note, for example, that although Parsons offered a number of technical objections to Durkheim's proposition concerning the referent of religious symbols, the very first objection he raised was that "perhaps no other proposition could awaken more instantaneous indignation in religious circles than this," for it is "objectionally 'materialistic.' "[12] It clearly implied that religious ideas are illusions. Having developed his argument that religious ideas refer to a nonempirical realm that is off limits to science, he concluded by declaring his argument to be a "vindication of the general views of partisans of religion."[13] Many partisans agreed. Some years later one of them, Prentiss L. Pemberton, hailed Parsons's recognition that "there are ranges of religious reality which are never illuminated by the spotlight of scientific focus" and expressed gratitude that Parsons "humbly leaves open ontological questions." He concluded that "religious devotees have in Parsons's action sociology a helpful and not a hurtful social science."[14] It is not true, however, that sociologists of religion never criticize anything about religion either. For example, Parsons has made it known that he has little use for some kinds of religion—Protestant fundamentalism and sectarian religions that make utopian demands.[15]

## THEOLOGICAL ELEMENTS IN THE SOCIOLOGY OF RELIGION

Whereas many sociologists now have doubts that their discipline can be entirely value free, most sociologists of religion still subscribe to the doctrine that science can have nothing to say about the truth of religious ideas and hence can make no theological judgments. This doctrine is based on the methodological principle that science cannot investigate that which is non-empirical. Like the doctrine of value neutrality, this principle has a rational core. Its rational core is the fact that science has no methods for directly measuring constructs that are held to have no material substance. No tests can be made of such propositions as "God exists" or "Mary was conceived without original sin." Moreover there are no ways to test propositions about past events of which no traces remain (e.g., Eve's encounter with the serpent), or about events inaccessible to the living (e.g., Voltaire's presence in Hell). But many religious beliefs *do not* qualify as non-empirical in any of these senses. Most religions contain a large number of ideas concerning the impingement of supernatural power upon human beings and their world. These

propositions are vital links between man and God. Judaism and
Christianity contain many propositions of this sort. Scientists are
perfectly competent to assess the probable validity of such ideas,
as the long history of conflict between science and religion in the
Western world suggests. But just as sociologists have been reluctant
to subject the major propositions of their theory of religion to
empirical test, they have also tended to overlook the fact that many
religious beliefs can be assessed by the methods of empirical science.
The spirit of detente has restrained them from examining what they
are quite capable of examining.

The reluctance of sociologists to undertake such examinations is
undoubtedly reinforced by the tendency of .modern theory to min-
imize the part played by cognitive interests in generating and sustaining religious commitment. Thus while he writes in *The Social
System* an encomium for "the contributions of modern science to
man's cognitive orientation to his world in general," as contrasted
with early Christian or medieval religious belief systems, which
would not be "cognitively tenable without the slightest modification
in the twentieth,"[16] Parsons and his followers have maintained that
it is a mistake to think that religious commitment is the result of
a single-minded search for truth. In fact, one of the central points
of *The Structure of Social Action* is that human actors must not be
thought of as if their orientations toward the world resembled those
of a scientist. Drawing heavily on Pareto, Parsons emphasized the
non-rational foundations of many commonly held beliefs and values. Although he recognized that there are cognitive elements in
religious ideas, he agreed with A. D. Nock's observation that people
"do not in general 'believe' their religious ideas in quite the same
sense that they believe the sun rises every morning."[17] Writing several years later, Kingsley Davis criticized earlier theories of religion
for concentrating on the question of whether "religious ideas represent reality." We now know, he asserted, that religion "includes
many things besides statements of purported fact.... Actually," he
concluded, "whether or not religious ideas are true is probably the
least important question for social science."[18]

The notion that the validity of religious ideas is a relatively minor
question for social scientists has played an important role in correcting the tendency of earlier investigators to assume that religious
ideas are nothing but the product of the human quest for an em-

pirically correct understanding of the world. This bias, which reflected certain rationalistic presuppositions deeply embedded in Western culture, supplied a very limited outlook on religion because it underestimated the significance of its expressive and normative components. This bias was especially marked in the works of nineteenth century anthropologists and has been correctly challenged by modern theorists.[19] By the same token, Pareto's analysis of the non-rational foundation of much modern thought called attention to the fact that a great deal of "belief" is informed by non-cognitive interests even in the West. Pareto's work reminds us that the interest in truth is strongly affected by other human interests.

Yet it is possible to carry this line of reasoning so far that it denies to the cognitive interest any role in influencing religious commitment. Christianity, for example, has traditionally placed a great deal of emphasis on the truth of its basic teachings. Although it has enlisted other human interests as well, it has implied that these other interests, e.g., the need for an ultimate triumph over suffering, can be served only by a religion whose teachings are valid in the cognitive sense of the term. As Alasdair MacIntyre has remarked, Christian theologians tend to treat Christian beliefs as "factual in a perfectly ordinary sense."[20] It is one thing to say that the desire for ultimate truth is not the sole motivation for becoming a Christian. It is another thing to say that a conviction that one has found such truth plays little or no part in generating or sustaining Christian commitment. Just as some versions of the doctrine of value-neutrality have ignored the role which non-cognitive interests play in scientific work, so the postulate that religion must not be understood as a solely cognitive enterprise has ignored the role which cognitive interests do play in religious life. Many religious people are convinced that there is a rational foundation for their faith. In this connection it is interesting to note that despite his support for Parsons's theory, Pemberton was disturbed by Parsons's tendency to consign "religious communication to ... *expressive* rather than *cognitive* patterns." He did take comfort, however, in Parsons's recognition that "the cognitive patterns of religion have their separate and unique realm."[21]

It is important to understand that although Parsons and his followers have stressed the non-rational elements in human action, they themselves have been firmly committed to scientific rationality.

They have tried to explain the non-rational in a rational way, i.e., in a way which to them has scientific merit. In doing so they implicitly deny the validity of the perspective which religious people have on their own faith. This can easily be demonstrated by recalling the sharp distinction Parsons drew in *The Structure of Social Action* between the point of view of the actor and the point of view of the scientific observer. The observer must have access to the actor's viewpoint, but he need not accept it as valid unless it passes scientific muster. As Parsons put it, "where there is an explicit symbolic interpretation of his actions on the part of the actor it need not agree with that which would be imputed by the observer." Parsons assumed that in most cases it will not. The observer must then have recourse to a "residue-derivation analysis to get at the fundamental elements," many of which may turn out to be "repressed sentiments or complexes."[22] This approach is graphically illustrated by Parsons's remarks concerning the analysis of magical action. "In magic," he writes, "the actor's subjective orientation is generally close to that of belief in the intrinsic efficacy of the operation, but to the observer it is more conveniently interpreted as an expression of his sentiments."[23]

Modern sociologists typically make use of this approach not only in analyzing magical beliefs but in analyzing religious beliefs as well. Let us imagine a research project designed to explain why some people become neo-pentecostals and how their lives are changed after their conversion. Let us also imagine that these converts repeatedly tell the investigators that the Holy Spirit has entered their lives and is providing them with a guidance and strength they had never known before. How seriously would the investigators take these claims? They would certainly report them, and they would probably not doubt their sincerity. But it is highly unlikely that the investigators would accept their subjects' reports as plausible explanations of why their lives had been changed. Instead, they would seek an explanation in terms of such familiar variables as family background, educational attainment, personality traits, and so forth.

Despite their formal avoidance of theological issues, sociologists do make claims having theological relevance. Sociological observers regularly substitute their own "scientific" perspective for the perspectives of religious actors. They implicitly claim to understand the basis of religious belief and action better than religious people themselves do. Sociological analyses of religion imply that religious faith does not arise in response to the "reality" perceived by religious people, but rather it arises in response to a different "reality" perceived by social scientists. This latter reality is the set of psychological and sociological factors to which we have already referred. Earlier social scientific theories of religion proclaimed that religious ideas are illusions. Modern theory tries to avoid the issue of truth, but in practice it fosters analyses that must appear reductionistic to anyone who takes religious ideas seriously on their own terms. Sociological explanations of religion have the effect of explaining it away. They carry the inescapable implication that religious ideas are not true.

As long as sociologists could believe that their analyses of religion were both value free and irrelevant to issues of religious truth, it was easy for them to conclude that they could separate their professional work from their personal views on religion. But as it becomes clear that no social science is value free and that sociology does have implications for religious truth, the separation is harder to maintain. It is particularly hard to maintain once it is discovered that modern theory implies that religion is a good thing but that religious ideas are false. Those who are hostile or skeptical toward religion are not distressed to learn that sociology undercuts the perspective of religious people. The problem these sociologists face is how a moral order must be grounded. Partisans of religion, on the other hand, face the problem of how a new way might be found to protect the credibility of religion itself. If social science is to support religious belief, it must abandon its pretense of theological neutrality. It must try to find some scientifically admissible basis for religious belief. Whatever the outcome of research, the relation between social science and religion will be different from anything we have known in the recent decades of detente.[24]

# 2. Sociology, Christianity, and Humanity

## Jack O. Balswick

Thomas Hobbes wondered if it were in the realm of possibility to discover any resemblance of good order or organization in human society. He characterized human society as filled with "continual fear and danger of violence" and human life as "solitary, poor, nasty, brutish, and short." While contemporary sociologists are still vitally concerned with the question Hobbes raised concerning the nature of social order, they have for the most part rejected his view of human nature as base, brutish, and self-centered. Likewise, most contemporary scientific models of society assume a basic orderliness as intrinsic to human social being. While some leave room for social conflict, they do not relate that conflict to a model of human being which views man-in-himself as a free agent acting in a selfish way.

Most contemporary models of society have been greatly influenced by the contrasting analytic and phenomenological traditions, both of which are variants of the same basic post-Kantian themes. Both start from Kant's distinction between "noumena" and "phenomena"—between things as they are in themselves and things as they appear in consciousness. Both traditions rejected Kant's notion of things-in-themselves; but neither reverted to a pre-Kantian position. Instead, they dealt with the concept of "things-for-consciousness." Most significantly, the analytic tradition has emphasized the *objects* of consciousness, while the phenomenologists have emphasized the *intentionality* of consciousness.

The primary influence of the analytic movement on the contemporary social sciences has been the attempt to apply the logical positivist strategy of reductive analysis to the methods of sociology

and psychology. This has been the case both among the hard core
behaviorists and among "positivists" in general. Behaviorism and
structural-functionalism are both models of human being and society which are based on the positivistic tradition. In these models
the human being is viewed as a determined object to be observed
"objectively." On the other hand, more recently developing models
of human being and society are based upon the phenomenological
tradition. In these models the human being is viewed as an unde-
termined subject who escapes scientific scrutiny; thus all observation is characterized as essentially "subjective."

In this essay these models of human being and society will be
critically examined in reference to a Biblical view of the nature of
human being and society. Then, based on a Biblical view of human
nature, the elements of an adequate model of society will be suggested as a vehicle for maintaining fidelity both to the Christian
revelation and the legitimate pursuits of social science.

## A CHRISTIAN VIEW OF HUMAN NATURE

Since a consistent Christian understanding of human nature is
necessary before a critical analysis of the adequacy of existing
models of society can be undertaken, we could easily become stalled
here in the mire of historical conflicts in theological formulae. To
avoid this, I will make my own position clear by asserting that an
adequate model of society must be based upon a Biblical view of
humanity in which human beings are seen as created in the image
of God but to exist as a distorted image of God. More specifically,
as pertains to models of society, a human being should be conceived
as: (1) an indeterminant being who can in part behave creatively
and spontaneously; (2) a self-conscious being who is capable of
goal-choosing activity; (3) a being capable of doing evil as well as
good; and (4) a being who is responsible for its own behavior.

To affirm these aspects of human nature is not to say that human
beings are not in a certain sense products of society. I am not denying
Durkheim's claim that society is a reality *sui generis* with a nature
of its own; however, men's and women's actions in society are to
a large extent determined by certain basic universal human qualities.
Society is both shaped by and limited in its effect by these qualities,
even though they are themselves subject to considerable cultural

variation and modification. Individuals and society are best seen as maintaining their distinctiveness in a dialectical relationship, where society is a human product, but nevertheless an objective reality, and human beings are social products, but not only social.[1]

## MODELS OF SOCIETY

Basic to scientific investigation are either explicit or implicit assumptions about the phenomena which are being studied. For the last three centuries the universe has been conceived as a machine, whose movements are precise and predictable, which can best be understood in terms of causal sequences. For a time humanity escaped being thought of as a part of this great machine (hence the "humanities" as distinct from the "sciences"), but finally human existence too came to be accepted as legitimate subject matter for study via the canons of causal models. Although behavioral scientists have never completely agreed in the extent to which they have assumed a mechanistic position, most have until recently taken positivistic or neopositivistic approaches in their work. In the past two decades, however, there has been a movement among humanistically oriented social scientists toward phenomenological and existential models of human being and society. At the risk of overgeneralizing, I will attempt to discuss most contemporary models of society as either *positivistic* or *phenomenological*. Two additional types of models of society, *conflict* and *symbolic interactionist*, will be discussed separately due to their uniqueness vis-à-vis the Kantian problematic.

### Positivistic Models

Positivistic models of society are generally either causal (mechanistic) or teleological (functional). In the 1940s George Lundberg popularized the causal model in sociology with his book *Can Science Save Us?*. Although his strict positivistic approach was a minority position, sociologists generally adopted some form of positivism and saw the method of the physical sciences as their ideal. Most contemporary sociologists who continue to assume a causal model of society are behaviorists. It is ironic that a psychologist, B. F. Skinner, has become the major proponent of a causal model of society as he has begun to argue for the application of the principles of operant conditioning to the societal level. Strict behaviorists like Skinner deny human personhood by denying subjectivity. Human beings are viewed as physical objects open to scientific scrutiny, and description is in terms of a causal model. Events external to the individual are said to determine the behavior of the individual.

In the 1950s, structural-functionalism became the dominant theoretical perspective in sociology. Such structural-functionalists as Talcott Parsons, Robert Merton, and Wilbert Moore offered some moderation in positivistic methodology. Nevertheless human beings continued to be viewed as objects for consciousness in a theoretical sense. In the teleological model of the functionalists the human being as a person was submerged. The human being was viewed as a "personality system" determined by the "social system." Society became the determining force, and the human being the determined object. Dennis Wrong has referred to the functionalist view of humanity as the "oversocialized conception of man."[2]

The functionalists share three assumptions about human being which negate human individuality and conflicts with other individuals. First, actors are assumed to have acquired and internalized certain dispositions (e.g., attitudes, sentiments) and to be subject to certain institutionalized role expectations. Second, actors are assumed to operate according to certain fixed psychological principles (e.g., the reinforcement principle). Third, actors are assumed to share a system of symbols and meanings which serve as a commonly understood medium of communication for their interaction. This is the assumption of "cognitive consensus." These assumptions have led to an emphasis on normative behavior or conformity. The human being is seen as a choice-making creature, but only within the realm of fixed values. Creativity is submerged. Societal integration is also emphasized, with conflict, deviance, and change seen as results of social disorganization rather than intrinsic social processes.

These positivistically based models of human beings and society share common errors from a Biblical perspective. First, they view the human being solely as a socially determined object. The behaviorists view the human being as completely environmentally determined; the functionalists view him as determined by societal roles, psychological principles, and a shared symbol system. According to the behaviorists, the concept of human freedom or choice is an illusion; the functionalists view human beings as seekers of goals determined by society. Both fall short of a Biblical view of human beings as goal-choosers. Both views are also impotent in their attempt to explain human alienation, conflict, and individual struggle. Since human beings are not seen in their unique humanness as having identities distinct from society, the problems of alienation, exploitation, and human conflict are seen as merely reflections of malfunctions in the environment or social system. Although much more could be said of the variance between the positivistic models and a Biblical view of humanity, in short: (1) They fail to conceive of humans as self-conscious beings who are capable of goal-choosing activities; and (2) they fail to account for humans' ability to do evil as well as good.

## Phenomenological Models

A wave of phenomenologically and existentially based models of human being and society has emerged in the past two decades. These models are largely a reaction to the dehumanizing effects of the positivistically based models. Rather than focusing on the human being as an object for analysis, they emphasize the intentionality of individual consciousness by focusing on the individual as the creator of meaning in a meaningless world. These phenomenological models include the labeling theory of Howard Becker, Harold Garfinkle's ethnomethodology, the sociology of the absurd proposed by Lyman and Scott, Berger and Luckmann's "social construction of reality," and the neo-symbolic interactionism of Erving Goffman.

These phenomenological models make some valuable contributions to an adequate model of humanity and society. They deal with human beings as *human* beings, subjective beings who behave meaningfully. They do not view human beings as completely socially determined, but emphasize human creativity in the social situation. They also view conflict and alienation as prevalent processes; however, these models likewise share some fundamental weaknesses which put them at odds with a Biblical view of human nature. First, human nature is viewed as a social construction. No ahistorical human nature is posited or possible. Humans are free to define and redefine their nature with no limits. A Biblical view sees humans as created in the image of God and thus having certain intrinsic characteristics which limit their behavior, whether recognized or not. Human beings, in other words, are not the sole producers of their natures. Even the process of self-determination is carried out within a medium with its own structure. Second, all systems of belief are considered to be arbitrary and socially constructed. In dissolving the Kantian dilemma of things-in-themselves and things-for-consciousness, phenomenologists focus entirely on things-for-consciousness and deny the independence of the created world.

Objects are not the sole product of symbolic interaction as these phenomenologists contend, for even symbolic interaction itself depends upon certain criteria for meaningful cognitive activity. There are certain rules which must be followed for any discourse to be meaningful, e.g., the law of noncontradiction. As a result of these weaknesses, the phenomenological models are guilty of having lapsed into an overly subjectivistic position. By viewing all knowledge in the social world (including that of the sociologist) as merely one arbitrary perspective, the phenomenologists have substituted "perspective" for knowledge.

### Conflict Models

Most conflict models of society are but a little less positivistic than behaviorism or functionalism; however, because they stress conflict—the antithesis of social integration as usually construed—they deserve to be discussed separately.

There are presently two dominant conflict models of society: (1) the dialectical model, inspired by Karl Marx; and (2) the conflict-functional model, drawn from Georg Simmel. Marx was an economic determinist who saw conflict inevitably arising within an economic system which propagates an unequal distribution of goods. Conflict in economic interests continues to be the explanatory springboard from which contemporary Marxist sociologists begin their analyses of society. Although, like Marx, he thought conflict inevitable in society,

Simmel viewed conflict as a reflection of more than just conflict of interest, but also of those arising from hostile instincts. . . . Simmel postulated an innate "hostile impulse" or "need for *hating* and *fighting*" among the units of organic wholes, although this instinct was mixed with others for love and affection and was circumscribed by the force of social relationships.[3]

Simmel's conflict model of society is built upon a view of human nature that is very consistent with Biblical concepts; however, a leading contemporary proponent of conflict functionalism, Lewis Coser, reduces his position to define conflict simply as lying "in the unequal distribution of rewards and in the dissatisfaction of the deprived with such distribution."[4]

Contemporary conflict models, be they in the Marxian or Simmelian tradition—or some combination of each—fail to suggest that the source of social conflict may in part reside within human nature itself. There are contemporary Marxist sociologists who recognize that human beings are more than just reflections of society; however it is interesting to note that when one self-avowed Marxist, Richard Lichtman, argues that although the self is social, it is *not only* social, he supports this view by quoting from *Simmel* rather than Marx.[5] Although conflict models provide an accurate *description* of society, they do not actually provide an *explanation* of this conflict.[6]

Somewhat parenthetically, I would add that not all conflict should be understood by Christians as something bad or as resulting from human sinfulness. I agree with Marxists who see value in conflict, especially attempts by oppressed groups in society to better their situations, as in the case of the civil rights movement, for example, or at least initially in trade unionism.

### Symbolic Interactionism

Symbolic interactionism stresses that the world of human experience consists of objects, where objects obtain meaning imputed through the process of human social interaction. An individual also gains a view of his or her "self" as an object via the process of interaction with others. Thus reality is socially constructed in the process of social interaction, and what is real to the individual *is* real, because it is *real* in its effect upon that individual. Society can exist and social organization is made possible because people share a common symbolically constructed view of reality.

On one hand, symbolic interactionism has been criticized as

merely a social behavioristic orientation which provides a positivistic model of society, but on the other hand, as an orientation which views society as consisting of indeterminate actors who are "creative" and "spontaneous." Lichtman and Fichter each claim that the principal contributor to symbolic interactionism, George Herbert Mead, taught a social behaviorism in which the individual was explained as merely being a product of society. Lichtman writes: "For Mead too, the self disappears. This may be vigorously denied but the truth is that the self as a self-conscious subject of its own existence is dissolved in Mead's extreme social behaviorism."[7] Fichter claims that Mead destroyed the distinction between the individual and the social aspects of human beings and hypothesized that the only true self is one that is "essentially a social structure and... arises in social experience."[8] Turner's more generous assessment of contemporary symbolic interactionism, however, balances these criticisms somewhat. He argues that this perspective makes the following three assumptions about the nature of man:

(1) Humans have the capacity to view themselves as objects and to insert any object into an interaction situation. (2) Human actors are therefore not pushed and pulled around by social and psychological forces, but are active creators of the world to which they respond. (3) Thus, interaction and emergent patterns of social organization can only be understood by focusing on the capacities of individuals to create symbolically the world of objects to which they respond.[9]

Most contemporary symbolic interactionists probably view the self as the product of society, but the individual as a possessor of a human self which is indeterminant and can act creatively or spontaneously once it has been socially produced.

## ELEMENTS OF AN ADEQUATE MODEL OF SOCIETY

The main purpose of this essay has been to examine critically the major existing models of society in light of a Biblical view of human nature and of society. All of the examined models have been found wanting in one respect or another, but the degree of nonconformity varies considerably. To attempt to construct a "Biblical" or "Christian" model of society is not only beyond the limits of this discussion, but it is also an undertaking that would deservingly be suspected by both secular sociologists and Christian theologians. I would like instead to conclude more modestly by suggesting some of the elements that should be included in an adequate model of society consistent with a Biblical view of human nature:

(1) *Humans as capable of creating symbolic meaning and thus their own view of reality.* Much of the emphasis within symbolic interactionism and in some of the phenomenological models is consistent with this statement. A symbolic interactionist model which stresses that the individual in the company of other human beings creates symbolic meaning is more consistent with a Biblical view of human nature than either a behaviorist or functionalist model.

(2) *Humans as not the sole producer of reality and of their own nature.* Not only do causal and functional models fall short here but, for the most part, so do the phenomenological and symbolic interactionist models. Phenomenologists view human beings as the sole producers of their nature. To be sure, they do not make the same mistake as the positivists in viewing human nature as the product of society, but they also do not view humans as having an intrinsic nature that reflects—in an admittedly "fallen" way—the image of God. Certain conflict theorists come close to viewing human nature as intrinsically posited; thus Lichtman states that: "Human nature is not unchanging, but it is false to hold that there are no lawlike connections among its aspects. . . . [I]t is precisely because there is a lawlike connection among aspects of human activity that any kind of foresight and planning, including socialist planning, is possible."[10] Whereas Christians and Marxists may agree on such things as the existence of an intrinsic human nature or an inevitable eschatology, however, the *contents* of such beliefs are vastly different.

(3) *Humans as free to distort reality.* The Marxist model is in obvious agreement with this statement, as capitalistic and other polarizing economic systems are seen to create a "false" consciousness or reality. Within the phenomenological model, however, there is no reality to distort; rather, humans are "free" to create their own reality. The inadequacy of the positivistic models usually results in reality being defined in culturally relative terms. Reality is

here seen as a product of society. The individual can "distort reality" or "be out of touch with reality" only in the sense that he or she does not share "reality" as it is defined by society.

In regard to the "free" in this statement, we could say that while phenomenologists do view humans as free (more free to create than to distort reality, however), positivists offer an environmental explanation for a person's distorting of socially defined reality. An adequate model of society would posit an actual reality which humans are able to distort because they exist in a state of separation or alienation from the God who created that reality.

(4) *Humans as partially motivated by selfish interests.* It is at this point that all of the models appear to fall short. Although it is true that conflict theory stresses the inevitability of conflict arising in society, this model does not offer a clear explanation of conflict as arising out of the motivational aspects of human beings. In his article on social scientific conceptualizations of human being, Fichter states that, "As far as I can discover, sociologists have no model to explain that man can do evil as well as good."[11] Fichter continues to observe that although this is viewed as a theoretical weakness by Dennis Wrong in his own classic article on the "oversocialized" view of man, Wrong himself offers no alternative model of human nature. A model of society that takes into account the fact that humans can be motivated to evil by intrinsic selfish interests has yet to be constructed by any sociology.

(5) *Humans as capable of justifying their selfish behavior on the basis of their definitions of reality.* Humans are not only capable of selfishly motivated activities, but they are also capable of defining reality in such a distorted way that they do not interpret selfish behavior as selfish. Most of the models take into account this ability of human beings to structure reality in order to justify or legitimize particular oppressive behaviors, but most of these same models, as I have just noted, fail to view humans as having some intrinsic "weakness of nature" responsible for the initiation of their selfish acts.

(6) Finally, an adequate model of society must understand *humans as in need of interdependence through shared meaning, while at the same time accounting for the pervasiveness of group conflict.* Such a model of society would be consistent both with a Biblical view of human nature and with the way human beings in fact interact in society.

# Part II. THEOLOGY AND SOCIOLOGY

# 3. Theology Lessons for Sociology

## Ronald J. McAllister

The impetus for this essay was the recognition that a great deal of attention in the study of theology is being given to sociology in general and to social theory in particular. The attention focused on Marx is a prime example of the trend noticeable in many theological arenas. In spite of his atheism, theology has discovered Marx and Marxism. This may be seen most clearly in the development of liberation theology—which draws deeply on Marx's insights. Gustavo Gutiérrez, a Peruvian theologian whose name is perhaps most often associated with this movement, observes that

Contemporary theology does in fact find itself in direct and fruitful confrontation with Marxism, and it is to a large extent due to Marxism's influence that theological thought, searching for its own sources, has begun to reflect on the meaning of the transformation of this world and the action of man in history.[1]

Furthermore, the "confrontation" of which Gutiérrez speaks has not been restricted to consideration by political or liberation theologians.

Significant attention to Marx and other social theorists may be found in the fields of ecclesiology, dogmatics, Christology, and so forth. The works of Hans Küng and Gregory Baum both deal extensively with Marx, Hegel, Freud, Durkheim, Weber, and others.[2] The awareness of social theory among theologians is presumed to reflect the impact of sociology on theology. Awareness of Marx and Marxism has become practically mandatory for theologians—

although one suspects that for some theologians reference to Marx is more faddish than substantive.[3] Nonetheless, theological attention to Marx is one gauge of the impact that sociology has had in recent years on theology.[4]

Some of the best work on the implications of sociology and social theory for theology has centered in Great Britain. Robin Gill's books *The Social Context of Theology* and *Theology and Social Structure* are important reading for anyone interested in the sociological understanding of theology as a field of knowledge. Both these books represent breaks with the once-common (especially in Europe) but now waning field of "religious sociology," which sought to use sociological ideas for the propagation and organizational success of particular religious traditions. These works focus directly on theology, seeking not to influence theology but rather to provide sociological analyses of theology and how it takes shape. In a way, these books begin to turn the tables on the main historic relationship between sociology and theology by constructing a sociology of theology.

From the point of view of the present essay, however, Gill does not go far enough. Here I am seeking an understanding of the ways in which theology might be of service to sociology and social theory. I want to go beyond the sociological study of theology and ask how theology might influence the course of contemporary sociological work. Before exploring the ways in which the two fields might interact, it will be useful to highlight some of the history of the relationship between the two disciplines.

## SOME HISTORY AND MODELS

Sociology has its roots in the same intellectual soil as theology. Theology may have a more direct concern to understand human nature, but the question "What is it to be human?" is an important one for both. The assumptions that each field makes about human nature, as Balswick suggests, are crucial determinants of the thrust and substance of the fields, but they are close in other ways too. Sociology originated in the attempt of Auguste Comte—and to a certain extent his predecessor, Saint-Simon—to dislodge theology from religion. The science of positivism was religion to Comte, who left the Catholic faith in 1811 at the age of thirteen and seems clearly to have been constructing its replacement with his "religion of humanity."

In the beginnings of sociology we see similar goals and constructions between religion and positivism. Comte had largely replaced love of God with love of humanity and salvation by God with human progress. While Comte's church in which sociologists would be priests and Comte himself the high priest never developed, the sociological enterprise has flourished in the time since then. In spite of the intellectual and historical closeness of the two fields, however, for most practitioners sociology is essentially a-theological and a-religious. This tendency is easily traced to Max Weber's discussion of value freedom (*Wertfrei*). The value free position and what Peter Berger refers to as "methodological atheism" are much more in the mainstream of sociological development than are Comte's ideas of a positivistic "church" of science. In fact, in most sociological camps a virtual state of siege has existed against theological notions. Although a rapprochement is occurring in theological circles, there has been little tendency in this direction among sociologists.[5]

The uneasy truce between sociology and theology has lasted for some time in spite of constructive efforts to end the stalemate. The publication in 1980 of Martin, Mills, and Pickering's *Sociology and Theology: Alliance and Conflict* represents a recent effort in this direction. Yet the tensions between the fields are clear within the chapters of even this book. Some scholars within each field seriously want dialogue, yet a great gulf remains between them. This essay suggests that a good part of the problem lies in the fallacious belief (common on both sides) that while sociology may be able to contribute to theological inquiry, theology has nothing to say to sociologists in their study of society. At the heart of my essay, then, is the contention that this commonly held belief is incorrect.

We can explore the relationships possible for these two fields by focusing on five different models that may be used to describe the interaction of any two intellectual disciplines. One of these models describes the relationship appropriate to sociology and theology. The five models for conceptualizing this are: (1) a-relational, (2) heuristic, (3) proximate, (4) unidirectional, and (5) confluent.

I term the first of these *a-relational* because it holds that there is no relationship between the fields; neither contributes anything to the other. This is probably how many practitioners see sociology and theology: substantively unrelated. Theology is, after all, a tool of religious faith. It is a confessional experience, formed within specific ecclesiastical camps. It is not typically a means of understanding general religious inspiration, which most would concede is a properly sociological question. Theology per se does not exist in the abstract. It is always implicitly Islamic theology, Judaic theology, Catholic theology, or the like. Some would claim, in fact—though too narrowly, I think—that theology is a distinctly Christian endeavor.

Sociology, on the other hand, while sometimes "sectarian," is generally "value free." Theology can never be "value free." Of course, we have come to understand that sociology is not so "free" either, but that is a point to which subsequent attention will be given. In the a-relational model, theology and sociology are seen to be so separate from each other in intent and method that they are irrelevant to one another. The relationship between them is rather like that between microbiology and astronomy. They are two fields in two totally different worlds of discourse.

In the *heuristic* model there is a little more relationship than in the a-relational one. In fact, as in the first type, no substantial relationship actually exists. The relevance of one field to the other is basically as a device to help one to learn. This is often accomplished through the use of metaphor or simile. There are ways, for example, that some of the principles of physics can be applied to the very different world of economics, such as when an economist tries to understand the behavior of the money supply and its effects on the stock market by making an analogy to "critical mass." Such applications are strictly heuristic. Some would say that theology and sociology are related in the same way: *un*related but for simile or metaphor.

The third way of understanding a relationship may be thought of as proximate. In a *proximate* model, two fields are seen to be in the same universe of discourse and to focus on the same objects. But they operate in isolation from one another. Any linkage between the fields is due to their common focus and not to any meaningful dialogue. One might consider the fields of geology and geography as a model case. Each of these distinct sciences is concerned with the earth, as is shown in their common prefix, but their work and tools are generally quite different. One deals with the structure of the earth, while the other is concerned with the human uses of the earth. Some would say that theology and sociology are related in this fashion, both concerned with human nature but essentially different enterprises better left different.

The *unidirectional* model may be seen to operate in the relationship between the fields of mathematics and engineering. What we see here is a one-way street with the influence flowing from one discipline into the other but not flowing back again. The suitability of this model for mathematics to engineering is obvious. Engineering would be impossible without mathematics—engineers must study math, but mathematicians need not study engineering. The same thing is true for most theoretical fields and their applied counterparts.

Those who hold that this is the appropriate model for understanding the relationship between sociology and theology easily can point to a number of topics studied by sociologists that subsequently have been proved to have an impact on theology. Among these would be: community, leadership, belonging, meaning, alienation, and others. The development of religious sociology noted earlier is precisely within this model.

The final model, that of *confluence*, is the one that this essay presumes to be most appropriate for understanding how sociology and theology can relate. In this model there is significant interpenetration and cross-fertilization. The premier example of this type of relationship is that characteristic of biology and chemistry. The mutuality of these two fields has been so great as to produce a third field owing equally to both parent disciplines: biochemistry. In this model insights that develop out of the conduct of one field are examined by the second field and passed back again. The development of a third field, while not essential, gives solid evidence of the confluence of disciplines. The relationship between sociology and psychology has some of this model in it. Out of this confluence we have a third field, social psychology (although many, admittedly, would suggest that what we have in reality is two related subfields of social psychology, one in sociology and the other in psychology). Still, the degree of interpenetration is considerable between these two disciplines.

Whether theology and sociology could at some point cooperate in the formation of a third field (sociotheology?) is an open question at the present time. There are signs, however, that such a field is emerging.[6] If this model is to be advanced, it will be up to sociology to open its doors to theological inspiration and conceptualization, since, as already shown, theology has already begun to listen to sociology. Opening the sociological doors to theological work implies somewhat radical shifts in the historical drift of sociology from Comte to Weber to Berger. But owing to the doubts that have arisen about positivism, the time now seems right for such developments to take place. David Lyon suggests that now "a strategic door is opened for sociotheological dialogue."[7] First, however, it must be clear that if sociologists are to learn from theology, we will need to have a better idea than is now current as to the theological landscape. We must know what theology is and is not.

## WHAT IS THEOLOGY?

From its etymology one could learn that theology is "reasoned discourse about God."[8] Thus, it would appear that a fundamental assertion at the heart of theology is the existence of God. This is fair and accurate as far as it goes. Yet what Rabelais referred to as *"un grand peut-être"* need not erect a wall between theology and empirical sociology. There are numerous theologians for whom the existence of God is an open question, elusive, unverifiable, problematic. Informed theologians and all people of reasoned faith cannot ignore Hegel or Feuerbach or Marx or Nietzsche or Freud. Yet studying them does not destroy faith and certainly has not destroyed theology. Theology has survived and gained from "religionless Christianity," "the death of God," "religious atheism," and "the secular city." The field has been deepened by the contributions of Bonhoeffer, Robinson, and Cox almost as much as it has by Tillich, Barth, and Rahner. Thus when it is said that "God" is the first assumption of theology, one must refrain from inserting into that assertion one's own picture of that God.

The various images of God that have been constructed over the centuries are seen through the sociological imagination as social constructions. This, in fact, is one of the major contributions of sociology to theology. Such constructions are, as Feuerbach would have it, projections. Yet as Küng has so eloquently demonstrated, to say this is not to say that they are only projections.[9]

The "names" of God also are important sociological data. It is sociologically significant that the world's religions have had in their histories sometimes very different and sometimes very similar definitions of and emphases upon the attributes and names of God. The images of God as "enlightened," "forgiving," "eternal," "transcendent," or "avenging" tell us a great deal about the society that generates the particular images in question. What they tell us about God is less important and certainly less verifiable.

It is clear that emerging discourse-types within Christian theology now of the poor, or the black, or the feminist God are potentially very powerful images. And who is to say that the images do not, in fact, tell us something about reality? Such assertions are matters of faith. Yes, theology believes in God; but knowing that, one actually knows very little. Perhaps it would be a more useful exercise to look at the way theology is organized, if sociologists are to prepare for dialogue with it.

The field of theology is ancient and vast, closely related to philosophy of religion, but distinctly different from it. In the traditional Christian schema, the field was divided into three parts: *Historical Theology* (including Biblical archeology and languages, historiography, scripture scholarship, and exegesis), *Practical Theology* (including canon law, pastoral theology, and homiletics), and *Dogmatic Theology* (including dogmatics, fundamental theology, and moral theology or ethics). This traditional division, however, no longer serves as an effective organizing scheme for the field.

As with most attempts to divide the world into tidy categories, there are parts of it that simply will not fit. Thus, in the classical scheme one is hard pressed to find a single rubric under which to consider ecclesiology, eschatology, hermeneutics, or many other subjects of interest to theology. Further, many emerging theologies (e.g., liberation theology) defy such categorization and so cannot be subsumed under one of the traditional categories. The fact of the matter is—as a popular theological dictionary expresses it— " 'theology' has become a generic term for a number of interrelated disciplines."[10] There is no longer a single theology within most individual denominations; theology should be considered a plural noun.

The question, however, is not the current turmoil of theology. Rather it is the relationship between sociology and theology and how the sociological enterprise might be advanced by the theological. Perhaps the most useful opening is within the field of moral theology, the relationship between sociology and ethics.

## SOCIOLOGY AND ETHICS

Bernard Häring, the renowned German ethicist, suggests the proximity of ethics and sociology when he offers the opinion that "the task of ethics begins where sociology ends."[11] I would suggest that the barrier between the two fields is not so rigid—or at least *should not be* so rigid—as his view implies. There is, instead, a floating zone of common interest for the two fields. It is within this zone that dialogue might most fruitfully take place.

Ethics, whether of the type derived in moral theology or the type derived in philosophy, has to do with "right behavior," which may in turn be seen as conformance to accepted principles and values. The thing that separates the theological root of ethics (say, as expressed in Thomas Aquinas) from the philosophical root of ethics (as in Immanuel Kant) is the *source* of the principles. For moral theologians such as Häring, right behavior may be traced back to revelation and sacred texts, while philosophical ethicists work apart from such faith contexts. For present purposes the distinction between the two is technical and irrelevant. Ethicists, whether of the theological or philosophical type, seek to understand what constitutes right behavior.

Sociologists, on the other hand, traditionally have rejected the idea of "rightness" in describing behavior. For the social scientist, behavior simply *is*. It should be clear, however, that this position—the value free position—is a part of the *ideology* of sociology (as Gouldner defined it over twenty years ago). To be value free is to be free to study what we want, but it also is to be free of responsibility. Our ideology is a way of escaping accountability. When we are value free, we are neutral; we cannot be blamed. Such a position is a justification for doing what we want instead of doing what we ought.

To raise the question of *oughtness* clearly opens the door to theological (or at least ethical) inquiry. "What ought I to do?" is one of two questions at the heart of ethics and at the same time a question that can prove crucial to modern sociology. The other fundamental question, "To whom (or to what) am I responsible?" is less often thought about in sociology but no less important. It is not as if these issues do not exist for sociology. They do. But for many social scientists they remain partially or wholly unaddressed, their implications only vaguely sensed.

Admittedly, sociology already asks the "oughtness" question in terms of the *conduct* of research. Over the last several years various codes of ethics have been developed by professional associations, including the American Sociological Association. These codes are designed mainly to answer procedural questions about such matters as informed consent, subject safety, invasion of privacy, the uses of research findings, and so forth. Although there may be some disagreement in specifics, furthermore, there is general consensus about right behavior in the conduct of social and behavioral research.[12] That this exists clearly indicates the wide-ranging acceptance of the limits of the value free concept. This, however, is only one part of the issue of "oughtness."

The more important part is the decision regarding what we *ought* to study in the first place. Here sociology has professed "academic freedom" and "value neutrality." But these do not make the problem go away. The question, "What ought I to study?" is the fundamental ethical question for social science, a question that moral theology can help to answer. It also may be that moral theology can help to answer (and at least remind us to ask) the "responsibility" question as well. To whom (or to what) is the sociologist responsible in the conduct of research? There are several answers possible: one's self, one's discipline, society, posterity, employers, or perhaps even the answer proper to the theologian. Our code of ethics provides one answer; yet the sense of objective truth that once pervaded our science has slipped away, leaving in its wake serious doubts about the ability of scientific knowledge to encompass any universal claims. In discussing the case against positivism, Küng, reacting to the work of the great philosopher of science Karl Popper, suggests that "logical positivism leads to absurdity," and that positivists "in their anxiety to annihilate metaphysics, annihilate natural science along with it."[13]

Social science seems to have arrived at this realization somewhat later than physics and the other natural sciences, but its impact here inevitably leaves us looking for certainty when there is none to be had. We once thought that by separating "science" from other disciplines and purifying scientific methods, we could distill a standard for measuring truth in the world. It is not so. Implicit here is a bifurcation of the world into camps typically labeled faith and reason or knowledge and feeling. It is this division to which Gouldner refers as the "minotaur," that mythological creature—half man and half bull—against which he so ably spoke.[14] The desire to separate science and religion, sociology and theology, is wrongheaded, unfortunately leaving both fields less than they might be were they free to work together.[15]

George Lundberg argued in the 1940s in an important little book that we should "render unto science the things that belong to science and to metaphysics the things that belong to metaphysics."[16] While his point is well taken, the rigidity of his compartmentalization of knowledge into *apartheid* camps must be questioned. His affirmative answer to the question *Can Science Save Us?* is wrong. If the twenty years before the second edition of his book appeared did not prove him incorrect, then surely the twenty years since have done so. Gouldner tells us that "Before Hiroshima, physicists also talked of value-free science; they, too, vowed to make no value judgments. Today many of them are not so sure."[17]

The question for us to consider is whether we can dedicate ourselves to the pursuit of truth when we are uncertain about what we ought to do and unclear about that to which we are responsible. These important value questions can be informed by theological discourse. The fields, as suggested, are not so far apart that they cannot affect one another as in the confluent model discussed earlier. This value area is just the place for theological input to sociology. A word of caution, however, is in order.

Although theology can legitimately provide stimuli for sociological research, it cannot dictate to sociology what must be done. It can suggest research to us but not conduct it for us. In suggesting that the fields can be close and should crossfertilize, I have not said that either of the fields should take over the other. They should not. They are different enterprises; yet, they can "overhear" each other, as John Orme Mills has said.[18] In overhearing, too, they may each inspire. A major vehicle for this inspiration in theology for sociology, I suggest, is the ethical questions of moral theology. Beyond these questions there are still other materials of theology that can inform sociological work. Two such areas of theological input are the *concepts* with which theology works and the *images* it generates.

## OTHER THEOLOGICAL INPUTS

Primary among theology's sociologically expressive concepts are "evil" and "sin." How can the sociologist understand these notions? Certainly it must not be in the individual sense. The sociologist has no proper interest in the behavior of an individual. Therefore, we look to structural evil and social sin. Historically, sociology has avoided the study of both of these routine theological topics—E. A. Ross's *Sin and Society* being the classic exception, but one little referred to today. Stanford Lyman traces some of the reasons for this sociological oversight in his remarkable book *The Seven Deadly Sins: Society and Evil.* Beyond his work and that of Ernest Becker, there are few sociological works dealing with the subjects.[19] Yet evil exists. In theology, it fashions "theodicy"; in sociology, "social problems." Our adoption of the *wertfrei* position blinds us to the negative cast of the problems that exist. We seek only what is true, blind to what may be evil. Thus we shy of the amelioration of evil, when consideration of its structural dimensions and their amelioration would be real advances in sociological knowledge as well as in the quality of social life. Here sociology can learn from theology.

The areas of conceptual input, furthermore, are not limited to the "negatives." Other concepts to which sociology might attend are, among others: peace, justice, providence, mercy, grace, and virtue—areas that are largely uncharted waters for sociological investigation.[20]

Another area in which theology can play a formative role is in terms of the images and metaphors upon which it draws. The imagery of the Apocalypse is one particularly rich example. In the Apocalypse we see the metaphor of the four horsemen, traditionally identified as *conquest, slaughter, famine,* and *death*—themes that could easily guide the sociological enterprise into important new areas, as well as enlarging the significance of older concerns. If a researcher wanted to move into other theologically inspired areas, one could inquire about four more modern horsemen, which might be identified as racism-sexism, technological imperialism, consum-

erism, and nuclear culture. These, too, could set an agenda for a
new sociology.

   Sociology, then, must learn to be in dialogue with theology, not
in submission to it—the mistake, perhaps, of earlier eras' conceptualizations of both theology and science. The theology lesson for
sociology is not in learning how to proceed—we are already clear
about the canons of our methodology—rather it is in knowing what
to value, what is important to study, and why. The willingness of
sociologists to speak and to listen now to value concerns is crucial.
To continue to follow the traditional social science response, declaring the discipline "value free" and backing away from theology
because of its non-rationalistic methods, its ultimate values, or its
pietistic bent would be a serious mistake. Theology offers something
to sociology. It gives the tools for an "ethic of responsibility" that,
for Max Weber at least, is to accompany *wertfrei* science.

## CONCLUSION

   The theological enterprise assumes that the values and actions of
individuals are shaped in light of what is understood about God.
It is out of the theologian's understanding of God, this God's relationship to people, and those people's consequent relationships
to one another that theologians do theology. Having a sense of
what is thought to be ultimately worthwhile (i.e., valued), the theologian deems it appropriate to speak about such global subjects
as peace, justice, liberation, violence, labor, hunger, and the arms
race.

   A great deal of recent attention in the theological community has
been focused, for example, on the subject of nuclear war.[21] In much
of this literature ethicists are making a case for peace special to the
nuclear age. A clear chain of assumptions exists for theologians
which permits them to take strong anti-nuclear weapons positions.
These assumptions generally lead to such a fundamental notion as
the "sacredness" of life. Under currently operating value free principles, there is no justification that a sociologist can fashion that
would allow any moral position to be adopted. Is peace better than
war? Officially, sociology has no answer. Is freedom better than
oppression? Scientifically, sociology is mute. Official, scientific sociology may know what is "true," but it has no capacity for re-

cognizing what is good. There is an irony here, too, inasmuch as the American Sociological Association and other professional associations within the social sciences *do* take moral positions, but have no basis for doing so other than members' "feelings."

Apart from the restrictive canons of the discipline, most sociologists probably think that justice and peace are important issues, while remaining less certain than theologians as to why. Within the discipline, value freeness has left us unfree to take a stand even on a question as basic as peace. This same lack of freedom affects the research we do—as well as that which we leave undone. The role of ideology in this cannot be ignored, and the sociologist is as restricted by the iron cage of ideology as anyone else. I suggest we admit this and move on.

There is no pressure here to adopt a single ethical argument. I have not said—nor would I want to—that sociology *is* theology, only that it can learn from theology. It matters little whether one takes Bonhoeffer's theology of Christian atheism, Gutiérrez's theology of liberation, Schumacher's Buddhist economics, or some other ground for developing one's research agenda. The more important issue is the decision to start from a position of important values. For purposes of fashioning a sociotheology, it is not important to distinguish Christian ethics from Muslim ethics—perhaps this is the sense in which Weber himself understood *wertfrei*.

It will make practical differences, of course, whether one draws one's background values from Aristotle, Jesus, Maimonides, Muhammed, Kant, Bentham, Marx, or Moon. But for the purposes of the argument I am making here, it makes no difference. The point is to use—openly—one's theology to construct a research agenda instead of letting it be set by whimsy, convention, or—worse yet, by the vagaries of funding agencies. To do so will be to do more important sociology.

# 4. The Sociological Theology of H. Richard Niebuhr

## William R. Garrett

H. Richard Niebuhr was one of the first theologians in the English-speaking world to make serious use of social scientific concepts in the twentieth century, as history had been employed in the nineteenth. Not only did these new tools extend out from a theological position to provide, as Niebuhr once put it, a means "fruitful for the understanding of a difficult situation,"[1] but they also fed back into that theological matrix where, at crucial points, they served to condition the theological task by defining the questions it posed and by structuring the responses which rebounded. The reflexive character of these newly acquired methods introduced sundry and troublesome problems for Niebuhr; nevertheless, he fully intended that these new disciplines should be firmly entrenched in an ancillary role whose function was to provide added support in the struggle to attain his primary goal—an effort to achieve greater theological intelligibility for a religious community confronted with an encroaching cultural aversion to the traditional concepts of the faith.

The social sciences proved a formidable ally against the dangers of embracing dogmatism of a supernaturalistic variety; but with equal force, the new sciences threatened time and again to tip toward an inundating relativism the precarious balance Neibuhr was seeking to maintain between these two realms. Niebuhr grappled with this hydra-headed problem as he sought to keep his social scientific infrastructure in line with his theological program. This essay will attempt to adduce evidence of the premise that, after a faltering start in *The Social Sources of Denominationalism*, Niebuhr later propounded in *The Meaning of Revelation* and subsequent

writings a form of theological argument that closely approxi-
mated—if it did not fully achieve—a sociological theology.

The line of analysis Niebuhr launched in *The Social Sources* and
rejoined from a different angle in *The Kingdom of God in America*
eventually culminated in the more sophisticated and proficient ideal-
typical model of *Christ and Culture*. The configuration of these
three studies reflects an almost dialectical progression in response
to a common underlying theme in his corpus, wherein he repeatedly
attempted to resolve the enduring question of what should be the
relative valence accorded the separate elements of material and ideal
forces inexorably conjoined whenever finite human beings enmeshed in historical particularity confessed faith in an absolute God
who transcended all cultural relativity.

Niebuhr's appropriation of social scientific concepts in pursuit
of theological insight was not confined, however, to this incremental
literature dealing with the singular faith-culture problem of Troelts-
chian origin. Overlapping the same time period, Niebuhr was engaged on other fronts with theological problems that lent themselves
to a similar pattern of crossfertilization between social scientific
concepts and theological doctrines. One sector where this method
paid handsome dividends derived from Niebuhr's reinterpretation
of the meaning of revelation. As in *The Social Sources*, a social
scientific infrastructure largely obscured by the manifest theological
issues of *The Meaning of Revelation* contributed decisively toward
the building of that constructive argument which Niebuhr was intent on adducing. The implications accruing from that underlying
social theory crucially affected the cogency of Niebuhr's analysis
and, by extension, the current evaluation to be accorded Niebuhr's
resolution of the problem of revelation.

## REVELATION AS SOCIALIZATION: NIEBUHR AND
## G. H. MEAD

*The Meaning of Revelation* (hereafter *TMR*) presents an ironic
paradox when compared with Niebuhr's earlier accomplishment in
*The Social Sources*. Niebuhr began his research there within a pur-
portedly sociological frame of reference; but scarcely after it was
launched, the analysis devolved into historical interpretation
grounded in the theoretical presuppositions of Progressive histori-

ans. In *TMR* the opposite procedure obtained. Niebuhr articulated the decisive categories of this study in terms of inner and outer history, and thereby set the stage for assessing the volume's cogency against the backdrop of his felicity at resolving the meaning of revelation amid expressly historical rubrics. The crucial insight undergirding Niebuhr's neoteric approach to the problem of revelation, nevertheless, had its genesis not in the historical but in the sociological domain, and more specifically in the seminal ideas of George Herbert Mead on socialization. Ferreting out the theoretical contribution of Mead in this instance will go a long way toward establishing the premise that *TMR* is preeminently an exercise in sociological theology.

Niebuhr introduced the concept of inner history as a bold departure for deciphering the nature of the revelatory experience without, at the same time, compromising either the transcendent status of Deity or the historically relative posture of the believer. At first glance, the process of inner history appears deceptively modest and uncomplicated. The possibility springs to mind that inner history merely represents a slightly refashioned version of Kant's pure practical reason, or perhaps a mild flirtation with the relativistic stance of historicism.[2] Again, there dawns a further possibility, founded on the references to Martin Buber's "I-Thou" perspective, that inner history may well consist of an eclectic synthesis of Buber's thought with these other ideational elements, a synthesis whose whole is greater than the sum of its parts. None of these alternatives, singly or together, however, adequately accounts for the polished rationality and structural symmetry Niebuhr effectively integrated into the notion of inner history. Kant's pure practical reason by dint of its eighteenth-century background, as Niebuhr incisively observed, failed to reckon very adroitly with the social and historical conditioning of the self.[3] Historicism took such cultural conditioning for granted, but it promptly encountered another range of difficulties associated with the troublesome phenomenon of a Divine Revealor who transcended the iron law of historical particularity. Finally, the elegant terseness of Buber's poetic philosophy revealed a vagueness at precisely the point where Niebuhr's internal history evinced substantive lucidity and amplification—namely, with regard to the empirical process by which the social self evolved within a communal context. Similarly, while Buber displayed an intrepid abandon to invoke mystery and a temerarious disregard for the restraints of logical consistency in his aesthetic description of the "I-Thou" relationship, Niebuhr demonstrated a countervailing interest in blazing a path through the tangle of inner and outer historical relationships which was empirically as well as scientifically credible.

The shortfall of these several factors to render a full accounting of Niebuhr's formula for inner history lends added support to the conclusion that some seminal input to Niebuhr's reflection still lurks below the surface undisclosed. The opening wedge to a recovery of this missing link emerges from a close comparison of *TMR* to Niebuhr's earlier writings. Such an examination divulges a striking new addition to Niebuhr's stock of analytical concepts, an addition that breaches a conspicuous void in his previous work. Carefully immured within the broader scope of the inner history notion, Niebuhr evidences for the first time a viable and sophisticated image of the self, and this theory of the self continued as an indispensable ingredient of his thought from *TMR* through the posthumously published essay, *The Responsible Self*. The intervening variable which turned Niebuhr's thinking around on this issue from his earlier vehement animosity toward "bourgeois individualism" in *The Social Sources* and prompted him toward a more sympathetic evaluation of selfhood was his exposure to Mead's perspicacious theory of the social self.

The dating of when Niebuhr appropriated Meadian theory admits only approximate reconstruction. No evidence of Mead's influence appears in Niebuhr's major writings before *TMR*. There is testimony from one of Niebuhr's students, however, that he first heard of Mead's thought in Niebuhr's lectures in 1940, or just a year before *TMR* was published.[4] Despite the curious fact that Niebuhr never cited Mead in *TMR*, the conceptual congruity between Mead's distinctive interaction theory of socialization with its doctrine of the social self and Niebuhr's detailed explication of the revelatory process-in-community mesh with such extraordinary synchronization that the coincidence simply cannot be dismissed by appealing to chance or happenstance. Certainly, Niebuhr's later writings overtly acknowledged the salient role Meadian social theory wielded in molding his thought.[5] The fact that Niebuhr laid increasing stress on Meadian social theory in his later writings, of course, has never really been at issue among Niebuhr's interpreters. What has not been systematically demonstrated in the secondary literature, however, is that Meadian influence prevailed in generous measure in *TMR*. Evidence in support of this proposition will not only serve to clarify the nature of Niebuhr's argument in this volume, but it will also provide a means for adjudicating the cogency through a goodly portion of that scholarly criticism addressed to Niebuhr's understanding of the process of revelation.

The distinguishing marks of Meadian thought find ample expression at numerous points in Niebuhr's carefully composed formulation of the doctrine of revelation. Perhaps the most notable illustration in this regard emanates from Niebuhr's fundamental proposition that Divine self-disclosure invariably occurs within a social context—within the movement of inner history which speaks from the perspective of participants to whom something has happened in community. The essential sociality of Niebuhr's approach effectively supplanted the subject-object dichotomy prominent in Western philosophical analysis with the self-other model developed by Mead and others in the Chicago School.[6] By reference to this model, a cluster of convenient criteria were furnished for eliminating several competing notions of revelation, and Niebuhr arrived at the conclusion that revelation represents an illuminative moment within inner history which gives rise to a special type of knowledge, at once deeply personal and ultimately valid, which differs qualitatively from the hard information acquired by objective, rational analysis.[7]

The overriding importance Niebuhr assigned to an ongoing participation in communal life as the *sine qua non* for the appropriation of religious meaning judiciously paralleled in a succession of crucial instances Mead's pioneering formulation of the socialization process. Just as Mead proposed in a secular context that selves, through their interaction with significant others, acquire a definition of and orientation toward reality replete with meaning, appropriate role patterns, and normatively binding value commitments,[8] so Niebuhr constructed the "story of our life," as he skillfully portrayed the form and substance of inner history, to encompass that social learning process by which religious signification carried by the community is introjected into the self as a foundation for religious understanding. Thus, socialization into the perspective of inner history constitutes the precondition for revelation, since the illuminative revelatory moment requires the inner historical frame of reference in order to be intelligible.

This structuring of his argument allowed Niebuhr to maintain vis-à-vis conservative and supernaturalistic theologians that revelation is not a sudden disclosure of divine content; it simultaneously legislated against the alternative danger (associated with the liberal stance) of reducing revelation to a numinal experience devoid of content.[9] Each self by virtue of its assimilation into the community of faith brings to the revelatory occasion a substratum of content conditioned by the social location and theological viewpoint of its religious group; yet in the revelatory moment, the self-in-community apprehends the Person of the Revealor who "patterns" and transforms the knowledge acquired from prior socialization. Hence, Niebuhr can properly declare that "by revelation in our history, then, we mean that special occasion which provides us with an image by means of which all the occasions of personal life become intelligible," while also steadfastly affirming that revelation is the handmaiden of reason, for "without reason revelation illuminates only itself."[10] Thus, the crucial function accomplished by the revelatory moment, the interactional encounter between the self-in-community and the "Deity of God," lies in the legitimation of inner history, which transvalues the knowledge acquired by socialization along with its attendant moral law into a more "extensive and intensive" application in the life of the self.[11]

Reduced to its most elementary forms, Niebuhr's proposal enjoins a series of discrete analytical elements including these salient features: (1) The knowledge held prior to the revelatory occasion is a lived inner history obtained by the self as a consequence of its socialization into the community of faith. (2) The fundamental modality for comprehending the bond of unity among self and community and God is understood in interactional and ongoing relational terms. (3) The "Deity of God" is specified through the category of "personalism" so that the interactional unity comprises a relation of persons—God and self and selves-in-community. And, (4) the revelatory encounter between the person of God and the self-in-community functions to legitimate and transvalue the self's prior knowledge of the faith; hence there is established out of this event a more intensively binding subjective commitment of the self toward the person of God and the religious knowledge carried by the community.[12]

In striking contrast to Buber, whose circumscribed definition made community a sometime thing, Niebuhr fully amplifies the ongoing function performed by the community of faith in the revelatory process—even to the point of arguing that community approbation furnished the regulatory base for discerning the validity of the experience itself. The fuller vision informing the fundamental features of Niebuhr's augmented view of sociality finds its orientation in Mead's stress on the social formation of meaning and the historical conditioning of all present action, both of which are finally rooted in an ongoing interaction sequence and intimately bound up with the process of socialization.

Meaning was for Mead emergent from the interrelation of selves wherein a gesture, understood in its most simplistic sense, or a verbal gesture, speech, called forth the same response in ego as it did in another organism toward whom the gesture was directed in the social act.[13] Meaning is always a social phenomenon whose existence remains predicated on a shared understanding obtaining between at least two—and usually more—selves. Thus, the stipulation Niebuhr formulated concerning the necessity for social corroboration validating the meaning of revelation adheres with remarkable conformity to the same ground rules Mead recognized for the establishment of meaning in general.

Meanings organized into mutually shared attitudes and expected action responses, furthermore, constitute the raw materials for Mead's theory of social roles and, thus, for role taking.[14] Unquestionably the most outstanding contribution generated by his innovative conceptual framework, Mead's role theory has commonly been understood to denote a distinctive set of "typified responses to typified expectations."[15] Of much larger significance for Niebuhr's refurbished notion of revelation, however, was the fact that familiarity with role expectations facilitates the "taking of the role of the other," even when those patterns include roles which ego may not legitimately appropriate *in actu* itself—for example, if ego is a child, it cannot function as mother or father, but it may "take the role" of mother or father, particularly in play, in order to understand and accept their attitudes and actions toward it.[16]

The role-pattern model for comprehending the relationship be-

tween interacting selves of sometimes quite different and mutually
exclusive statuses opened up whole new vistas for Niebuhr's reflection. By conceiving the revelatory interaction in terms of Meadian role theory, *mutatis mutandis*, Niebuhr was presented with a
structural mechanism for articulating the nature of the I-Thou encounter, a mechanism that fully protected the unique integrity of
both persons in the interaction-set. This model also facilitated an
understanding of the didactic function occurring within the revelatory occasion wherein the self comes to grasp an altered perspective on reality disclosed when it glimpses reality from the
vantage of Deity. Finally, this relationship conduced, in turn, the
appropriation of a normatively binding attitudinal orientation along
with relevant role expectations commensurate with the renovated
reality structure perceived in the revelatory occasion.

  While holding firm that no new supernatural content is unsealed
through the revelatory encounter, Niebuhr now also asserts that a
form of knowledge is generated from the quality of the relationship
accruing between the believer and Deity. The perspective of God
toward the world of persons is faithfully disclosed in the revelatory
relationship. Revelation becomes, then, modestly analogous to
"taking the role of the other," in the sense that selves acquire an
understanding of the perspective of Deity. What the believer takes
away from the revelatory relationship is a transvalued outlook on
religious reality founded on an apprehension of the attitude disclosed by the Infinite Person who reveals Himself as intractably
committed to the self in the frailty and strength, transgression and
piety, belief and doubt manifested by the believer.[17] The overawing
experience of apprehending the Person of God, the perception of
God's attitude toward the self, and the modified behavior accom-
panying that perception, leaves in its wake an assurance of the
essential truthfulness and trustworthiness of an ongoing relationship in which the person has come to know himself to be known,
loved, and valued by the Absolute Other responsible for initiating
the union. So it is that Mead's doctrine of role interaction served
as a fundamental structure undergirding Niebuhr's view of the revelatory encounter. By reference to the implications derived from
this role model, Niebuhr was afforded the means of defining the
kind of knowledge developing within this vital relationship.

  Moreover, it was at the juncture where Mead integrated his concepts of role and role-taking into the social learning process of socialization that the "historionic tendency" entered into the sweep of his thought.[18] This process proved absolutely indispensable for Niebuhr in his effort to wrestle with the complex problem of the historical and cultural conditioning of the self in relation to the revelatory experience. The attainment of selfhood, Mead maintained, hinged on the ability of the organism to recognize, inculcate, and function—as both subject and object simultaneously—within the role categories furnished by the primary groups of which it was a part.[19] Over the long stretch of interaction with significant others and reference groups present in his community, a social field of common meanings as well as an organized character structure is gradually developed for the individual as a basis for selfhood. The self emerges out of the socialization process, consequently, intimately molded and its perceptions trenchantly conditioned by the unique historical and cultural location enjoyed by those primary groups fate has destined as its socializing agents.[20]

By arguing in this fashion, Mead not only ventured into a brilliant new frontier for understanding the social formation of the self, but he also laid himself open to the charge of having reduced the self to a mere function of social factors. He sought to mitigate somewhat the excessive significance accorded the community in shaping personality through the socialization process in his scheme by urging that the self may effect a feedback toward modifying the community that initially molded him. Creativity, societal reconstruction, progress, all spring from the action of discrete individuals who challenge the immediate situation of their societies with fresh proposals that must then win the approbation of others in the community before they can become actualized.[21] Nothing short of a moral duty, Mead continues, redounds to the self propelling the person toward a transcendence of the limited viewpoint of parochial groups and the achievement of more universal aims.[22] This accentuation of the role historical experience exerted in delimiting the options entertained by the self in the present shines through as a silent affirmation that illuminated Niebuhr's efforts to decipher the historical problem attending revelation.[23]

Extrapolating from the position of Mead, Niebuhr arrived at the conclusion that socialization into the inner history of the community of faith set the perimeters for the revelatory occasion as the self responded in light of the historically and culturally conditioned knowledge carried by the community. There emerges in Niebuhr's adoption of Mead's notions of role theory and socialization, then, a conceptual "fit" between the believer's encounter with the Absolute Person of God and the ongoing relativity of humans' historical knowledge inextricably rooted in the finite structures of human social existence.

It was by dint of this enduring sociality that Niebuhr cautioned against the temptation of setting down *the* definitive "meaning of revelation" in a once-and-for-all form. The process of revelation, as with any historically continuing interaction sequence among selves, encounters the inherent tension and warfare between such counterposed tendencies of structure and dynamic, form and change. Much in the same manner as Mead understood the problem of secular social change—the endemic conflict between the need for securing established social forms and the countervailing need for historical development, reevaluation, and creative transcendence[24] —so Niebuhr believed that revelation predicated on the responses of selves to the God of their destiny would evince progress, development, metamorphosis, and a kind of permanent revolution in the religious life.[25]

## PROBLEMS FUSING SOCIAL THEORY WITH THEOLOGY

Appreciably, Niebuhr was forced to introduce some stringent modifications in Meadian role theory before this sociological construct could become fruitfully amenable to an analysis of the revelatory process and illuminative of the divine-human encounter. The largest innovation turned on the qualification expounded relative to the face-to-face primary group engagement which had figured crucially in the manner Mead had conceived the interaction-set. Primary group relations made excellent grist for the Niebuhrian mill that transformed socialization into the doctrine of inner history, but the operation did not run as smoothly when Niebuhr turned to an application of role theory as a means of amplifying the finite-Infinite encounter.

The central difficulty inhered in the stubborn fact that God is not a Self like other selves. As Niebuhr incessantly reiterated, the Person disclosed in revelation is Unique, more than the God of philosophy and history, more than our self-justifying noble ideals and moral laws wherein we "disguise our transgressions by a vast self-deceit," more than the attributes we ascribe to God to quench our quest for ultimate order, first cause, or absolute being.[26] Our knowledge of God, rather, is first and foremost the knowledge of a Self, and this knowledge is acquired by a different form of knowing than all other forms.

Coursing through his poignant prose there is the recurring theme that the Infinite Person reveals his nature as a self, not because humans are selves and could apprehend God in no other modality, but because God is personhood in its most perfected form, that Self who in his goodness and power makes all other selves valuable.[27] Yet, the *sui generis* Selfhood of God whose uniqueness and activity transcend the routine interaction of day-to-day encounters violates the *sine qua non* of ongoing intimacy by which selves come to know others in all secular contexts. Thus, the query thrusts itself forward, forcing one to wonder whether role theory applicable to the finite realm can handle the interplay between finite and Infinite beings. By what criteria do finite selves familiar only with other finite selves discern the nature and Selfhood of the Infinite Other?

Less risk was associated with Niebuhr's procedure than appears at first glance, however, by reason of the assumptions undergirding the role theory perspective. Even when concerned only with finite reciprocity, the self, according to role theory rubrics, was understood to disclose that about the person which it chose to reveal. Role theorists have explicitly recognized that selves always retain a measure of privacy into which no one can penetrate by force. From this follows an ancillary conviction of even larger significance: Role theory has never assumed that the self, even in its undisclosed aspects, is fundamentally different from the behavior it manifests in ongoing action. In marked contrast to psychoanalytic theory, which has persistently strived to plummet the innermost depths of the individual psyche and reveal the "true" self lurking below or behind its appearances, role theory has resisted the temptation to develop a hermeneutic for such purposes, because it has never assumed that a "real" self lies behind the phenomenal self to possess an essentially different nature from that evidenced in action. Infused with the realistic perspective, then, role theory has consistently denied, for example, that a person may be essentially law abiding but behave like a criminal, or basically moral but persistently act immorally, or truly altruistic while manifesting selfishness. A person is what that person does, role theorists have maintained. Although a self may surely change from criminal to law-abiding citizen, or vice versa, there always remains an intractable coincidence between "who one really is" and what one consistently does. Of course, role theorists have not been so naïve as to assume that a self cannot on occasion "smile and smile and be a villain," but they have characteristically placed a heavier premium on the probability that eventually "the truth will out." They find the position infinitely more credible that intimate interaction will separate with methodical accuracy those roles which the self has genuinely inculcated from those which it has merely manipulated for the achievement of discrete, limited ends.

Armed with this stalwart canon of role theory, then, Niebuhr could proceed into the controversy over the meaning of revelation by pressing the argument that the Divine Self, like other selves, discloses only the knowledge that He chooses to reveal; yet this knowledge is ultimately trustworthy, for He has manifested Himself in a similar fashion to other believing selves in the past and present. Furthermore, role theory would urge that while Deity may be more than He has revealed Himself to be, we may nevertheless invest utter confidence in the conviction that Deity is not constituted of a different nature from that goodness and power by which He has made Himself known to the eyes of faith—for presumably, God enjoys a coincidence of nature and action, personhood and behavior, similar to that of other selves. The qualitatively differing natures separating the Divine from the finite self do not present an insurmountable problem to role theory nor confound the logical capacity for this theoretical structure to function in an analogous role. To the contrary, Niebuhr appears to have concluded that role theory evinces a certain felicity for balancing with proper delicacy the differences between finite selves and the Infinite Other, as it meanwhile thrusts forward a positive model for according reliability to the knowledge acquired from the revelatory encounter.

From what this analysis has disclosed, moreover, it appears at the current juncture that Niebuhr's argument from an analogy of sociological design did not frustrate the central thrust of his theo-

logical confession. Unlike *The Social Sources*, the theoretical infrastructure of *TMR* never challenged the hegemony of his
theological vision. Niebuhr's irreducible assertion that God is a Self
remained a theological affirmation through-and-through. Only after
this proposition was established did Mead's sociological model enter the picture to flesh out the positive implications of this pene-
trating religious insight. Perhaps the happier accomplishment of
this study owed a great deal of its success, then, to Niebuhr's earlier,
faltering experience. At any rate, Niebuhr became uncommonly
sensitive to the deleterious results that could accrue from intro-
jecting a secular idea system—philosophical, historical, or social
scientific—into the religious realm as a means for structuring a
theological confession. The conspicuous absence of references to
Mead in *TMR* may derive, at least in part, from Niebuhr's fear
that pressing fully into view his theoretical infrastructure might have
focused more attention on method than on the fruits which that
method was designed to bear. Surely had the name of Mead figured
significantly in *TMR*, Niebuhr would have been embroiled in a
controversy over whether his notion of God was not really Mead's
"generalized other" writ large. Niebuhr in fact resisted this obvious
possibility from Meadian thought and pursued instead a more sophisticated application of socialization, role theory, and the notion
of a social self.

## THE CASE FOR DEVELOPING A SOCIOLOGICAL
## THEOLOGY

The central issue to be addressed in this concluding section concerns the broader issue of the propriety of appropriating social
scientific constructs for framing theological discourse—namely, that
sociological theology represents a mode of analysis equally as ef-
ficacious for propounding a viable theological position as philosophical or historical rubrics. That is to say, no *a priori* grounds
exist for excluding social theory from an adjunct role in theological
scholarship, as long as one necessary qualification is satisfied: The
hegemony of the theological discipline must not be compromised
in the process of assimilating social scientific concepts into its comprehensive analytical structure.

Herein lies the crucial and distinguishing difference between the

sociology of religion and what I have termed sociological theology. The sociology of religion is an attempt to study religion objectively, by means of a conceptual frame of reference and "vocab-
ulary of analysis," which allows the social scientist to penetrate
into the meanings, social organization, and cultural consequences
of particular religious organizations or the religious institution generally, in relation to cultural processes.[28] The theologian, by contrast, begins with a faith in the "sacred" and tries to work out in
systematic categories the implications of this faith for human existence.[29] Sociological theology stands squarely within the second
camp. Its starting point is constituted out of a constellation of faith
affirmations that are enunciated and systematically expounded with
reference to sociological categories in lieu of more conventional
historical or metaphysical conceptual systems. The compass and
aim of sociological theology, therefore, remains decidedly different
from that of the sociology of religion, with which it may share some
common conceptual paradigms. However much each tradition may
press toward the same religious phenomenon at the center of its
analysis, their ultimate conclusions must necessarily be divided
across an unbreachable chasm, for the one bespeaks the language
*of* faith, while the other speaks, perhaps with the same language
but from a markedly different perspective, *about* faith.

To clarify my intention more precisely, sociological theology is
not to be construed as a call for reviving that spurious quasi-dis-
cipline labeled "Christian Sociology" which sprang out of the well-
meaning efforts of socially activist churchmen who previously la-
bored under the Social Gospel banner. Indeed, even during that
earlier era, not everyone understood quite the same thing by this
hapless phrase.[30] Tacitly immured among the legitimate concerns
of these earlier movements, however, there often abided the vain
hope that sociology might diffuse some scientific credibility to a
belief in God and thereby help facilitate the accommodation of the
church to a newly acquired scientific ethos. The sociological theology proposed here holds out no such expectations. Scientific credibility should no more be expected to attach to sociological theology
than to philosophical or historical theology. Sociological theology
is not presented as a means for mitigating either the necessity for
or the scandal of faith.

Whether sociological theology might not provide a more relevant
and meaning-laden mode of theological conceptualization for the

present era, however, remains a lively question for further exploration. The general diffusion of sociological language throughout the wider culture as well as the empirical, anti-supernatural, and pragmatic orientation of modern man lends credence to the suspicion that contemporary churchmen might more readily cathect with theologizing in a sociological mode than in more traditional metaphysical modes. Only the operationalizing of this supposition will finally verify whether the beckoning path to sociological theology winds its way toward a productive breakthrough or a barren desert for theological reflection.

By pleading the case for a sociological theology and by grounding this argument in Niebuhr's innovative reflection, however, I would be intellectually remiss if I did not admit that Niebuhr never conceived of himself as a precursor to a new school of theological discourse, nor in his self-effacing manner, would he have probably felt comfortable wearing the mantle of a prophet preparing the way for a new form of theological method. Undoubtedly, a major reason why Niebuhr has enjoyed such a lengthy train of admirers, but so few have aligned themselves with the stringent norms of his tradition, stems from the rigorous example he set for all who would follow his lead into new heights of theological exploration.[31] Hence, it would be neither a fitting tribute to Niebuhr nor an asset to the current deliberations of the church at large if the impression were left that the sociological theology advocated in this writing could be achieved by the facile wedding of "pop" sociology to a slipshod theological consort. The church in recent years has already witnessed aberrant theology in such generous portion that it would be unreasonable to expect this institution to endure with patience yet another foray into the depths of theological absurdity.

Sociological theology, therefore, is not merely another label for the secular or political theology of recent vintage that garnered so much public attention as it sought to address a host of volatile issues in the social domain. Rather, sociological theology takes for its mandate the translation of the central symbols of the faith into categories of sociological origin as a means for affirming and making intelligible the reality of God's being-for-humanity. Quite clearly, even a partial fulfillment of this ambitious undertaking requires an exertion of the keenest intellect that the responsible self is capable of mustering.

# 5. A Sociological and Fraternal Perspective on James M. Gustafson's Ethics

## Paul M. Gustafson

For as long as we have both lived, James M. Gustafson has been my brother Jim. We have also both pursued careers in religious studies: he as an ethicist, I as a sociologist of religion. In order to avoid the confusion of two Gustafsons and to maintain my deep personal involvement in this paper, I will refer to James M. Gustafson in the way I know him best, Jim.

Having read Jim's work and having heard and read critiques of it,[1] I have had the nagging feeling that there was a need for a sociological analysis of it. In particular there was a resonance from the work of Max Weber.[2] They faced the same problems as they struggled with ethical questions but arrived at different answers. It is my intent to develop the reasons why this similarity of problems but difference of answers occurred.

Weber sought through the study of the histories of civilizations to understand the emergence of the modern Western world. Of signal importance to his analysis was the development of rationality. As ethics is a significant aspect of culture and Weber was preeminently a sociologist of culture, he developed the implications of this rationality to a changing "rationalization" of ethics in the West.

Jim, living and working within the framework of modern Western culture and the knowledge gained through the application of Western rationality, need not be as concerned with the developmental process, but accepts the "now" as given. The sociocultural setting for any ethic, thus, is of great importance, as is indicated by the first chapter of Jim's *Ethics from a Theocentric Perspective*, the central work (as a whole) around which this essay will focus.

## THE WEBERIAN PATTERN

In sharpening his conception of post-Reformation Western Christianity, Weber used Asian salvation religions to systematize two worldviews as ideal types: the Western, theocentric; the Eastern, cosmocentric. For our purposes, we need only be concerned with the former. Wolfgang Schluchter suggests seven core differentiating characteristics within it:[3]

1. *Content of worldview*: A transcendent personal creator; human beings are God's special instruments.
2. *Theoretical solution of dualism*: Predestination.
3. *Practical solution of dualism*: Acting in the world to realize God's will.
4. *Cognitive component*: Historical metaphysics.
5. *Evaluative component*: Faith-oriented ethic.
6. *Expressive component*: Ethically conditional charisma, ethical prophecy.
7. *Relation of cognitive and evaluative components*: Evaluative component has precedence over cognitive component, a tendency toward practical rationalism and anti-intellectualism.

There is an "elective affinity" between the theocentric worldview and the method of salvation. It is *asceticism*, either inner- or otherworldly oriented.

### General Background for the Weberian Position

For Weber, a general value must and does exist. Values become institutionalized, become objective, making demands as value judgments, which have a validity different from cognitive judgments. One cannot be derived from the other. Values must be actualized in response to their claims and to the value interest of the responder.

Weber understood humanity to have a nature of dual "interests"—material, concerned with well-being, health, and happiness; and ideal, concerned with the search for meaning or "salvation." These interests govern action, mediated historically, interpreted and institutionalized. Through this last, our interests find a socially relevant solution: at the symbolic level in worldviews; at the level of action, in social structures. Together these provide a social order.

From a more empirical, historical position, the world is made of partial orders and worldviews. We understand social orders because they have symbolic components. Inasmuch as there is an evaluative internal meaning, then, orders have an ethical element as well as external instrumental aspects. Thus a social order has to be seen from both its ethical viewpoints and their fusion into a worldview, and its institutions and their overall structural integration.

## The Weberian Developmental Approach to Ethics

An ethic is *normative* when the rule for behavior is based on social expectations for *specific conditions*. It is *principled* when the rule is abstracted from a range of particularistic circumstances and imbedded in a *universalistic* metaphysic that is either religious or secular (e.g., natural law). The ethic can be adhered to because of external pressure (the "force" of law), internalized as an "ethic of conviction" of the right of the principle, or—later on—adopted reflexively, through a dialogic decision-making process.

In developmental terms, the crucial point for the appearance of a true ethical system was when religions developed from monistic magic to a metaphysical world which was dualistic, making possible a differentiation in causality—natural or ethical. A religious ethic comes first, but with further differentiation there develops an autonomous secular ethic, expressed particularly in political and economic terms. Salvation religions, being dualistic, had to find answers for "the need to compensate for the inadequacy of life in this world."[4] With enhancement of selfhood, it became more difficult to locate compensation in a world beyond; only the future of this world remained. Theodicy became anthropodicy, and the ethic of conviction was confronted by an ethic of responsibility, by the conflicts between the nearly autonomous multistructured units of Western society, with the dialectic of ethics, power, and law. "[I]nstrumental knowledge and enlightenment are equally important for the ethic of responsibility. It requires knowledge of means-ends relations and consequences as well as the results of value analysis. It requires exchanges between the evaluative and cognitive sphere which are still possible under the condition of modernity."[5]

Methodologically the ethic of responsibility is based on reflexive principle. It is "the transition from principle to reflexive principle,"

Schluchter claims, that is "the decisive step" from the ethic of conviction to that of responsibility. It is the reflexive, dialogic process, which brings the individual back into the process of developing an ethic, not a mere personal morality, since in the reflexive process one must take into consideration a variety of principles as well as the consequences of one's own actions for others.

## THE GUSTAFSON PATTERN

### Jim's Theocentrism

Jim retains a theocentric conception of religion, but one quite different from that abstracted by Weber. This is due partially to differing purposes. Weber was concerned with the differentiated religions and their impact on the general culture, polity, economy, and the like, in seeking answers to the particular development of Western society. Jim's concern is to perceive the more universal elements in the understanding of God and then to view it in the more particularistic perspective: "God is the God of Christianity but God is not a Christian God for Christians only."[6]

Having said this, we can examine Jim's work with respect to each of the Weberian dimensions of a theocentric religion:

1. *Content of worldview*: A transcendent creator, but to be understood beyond the usual anthropomorphic vision of Him, who is *ordering* the universe. *One* source used by Him is humanity.

2. *Theoretical solution of dualism*: A rejection of predestination, what Weber assumed was the rational theodical answer. I have found no clear statement on this, but if (as Jim insists) God is God of the universe, not merely of humanity, even the issue of dualism is blurred.

3. *Practical solution to dualism*: Jim concurs that it is humanity's duty to realize God's will by acting in this world, but on the base that a human is a bio-socio-psychological unit with a *natural piety*,[7] which may or may not be oriented to God.

4. *Cognitive component*: He includes historical metaphysics and ideologies, but of particular importance are the modern sciences—physical, biological, and social. There is an implied ecclesiology.

5. *Evaluative component*: Jim rejects the use of the word "faith" because of recent accretions to and deletions from its meaning. He chooses

"piety" in its earlier meaning; so the phrase becomes "piety-oriented" ethic.

6. *Expressive component*: Jim's universalistic perception of religion and his broad-based knowledge of the social sciences find religion can be expressed in all human interaction, in the natural world as well; thus he would include charisma and ethical prophecy.

7. *Relation of cognitive and evaluative components*: The evaluative component is very important, but an enhanced awareness of the cognitive is needed.

In my life, Paul, it is trying to be a faithful religious person in the midst of an exceedingly high-powered aggressive community of intellectuals in whom . . . I discern profound religious sensibilities and . . . moral sensitivities that put most of the churches to shame. . . . I am not only concerned with the resymbolization of Christianity so that these traditional symbols can be meaningful. . . . But I am concerned that we recognize a certain kind of authenticity, a religious sensibility and moral profundity and sensitivity and . . . find a way of talking to that, of nurturing that, of helping that become self-critical, and of not building barriers . . . to the ultimate that life is about, which is (not) preserving that damn tradition but it is service to God.[8]

In this quotation we see Jim's strong concern for the cognitive element and also a concern for the total response of a person. His tendency is toward a practical rationalism, but it is certainly not anti-intellectual. He is strongly inner-worldly ascetic,[9] consonant with his insistence that modern scientific knowledge is an aspect of human participation in God's ordering of the world.

## Jim's General Background

Although Jim does not develop a particularized theory of values, I find a great deal of congruence with the Weberian position. Ethics, inherently evaluative, makes values central to the ethicist. That there are value systems in conflict in modern societies, which in turn predicate ethical responses, is the basis for Jim's as well as Weber's ethic of responsibility based on reflexive principles. Jim's recognition of ambiguity as inherent in all religio-moral situations is attuned to the Weberian emphasis on variances in values in cultures through time.

Jim, writing in the now of the world, accepts many of the elements spelled out by Weber as he developed his analysis of the Western worldview. Values become institutionalized, make objective demands on us. Values have other bases than cognitive, thus value judgments and cognitive judgments, interrelated but not the same, cannot be derived from one another. Consciousness of self is very much a part of modern life. For Jim, the dead weight of much traditional Christianity[10] and the institutionalization of values[11] are stumbling blocks to responsive ethics and its reflexive process.

Unlike Weber, Jim has a profound relationship to God. In it he recognizes the condition of the world and can opt for the same responsive ethic Weber calls for, but with a different outcome. Our ethic need not be lonely, we can relate to God, if we orient our natural piety to Him, giving us a conviction as support, and through Him fulfill our social being, not limited to rationality, through relationships with others. There is hope.

## Jim's Social Order

Jim's position is explicitly that of the social scientist's understanding of human beings and their activities.[12] Like Weber, he is a nominalist; he starts with persons as actors. They build structures that act back on them, more explicitly than Weber stated. Jim is reminiscent of Berger and Luckmann in *The Social Construction of Reality*, but with a Durkheimian touch. Jim does not make as sharp a distinction as to the duality in human nature, nor does he see as much autonomy in the various social institutions and value spheres. He certainly accepts the Weberian distinction between material and ideal interests as real, but he sees a greater degree of integration of institutions and spheres.

Weber's basic unit was the *meaning* of the act, derived from the culture, social structure, and personal experience. Meanings are importantly symbolic. Abner Cohen in *Two Dimensional Man*, arguing that humans live in two orders, political and symbolic, defines symbols as "objects, acts, relationships or linguistic formations that stand *ambiguously* for a multiplicity of meanings, evoke emotions and impel man." They are grouped as dynamic ideologies or worldviews. Just as different symbolic forms may have the same kind of symbolic functions, the same symbolic form can

serve many symbolic functions; yet "by objectifying roles and relations, symbolism achieves a measure of stability and continuity
without which social life cannot exist."[13] Both Weber and Jim recognize this. Both see religion as the historically most important
system, yet a changing one. Weber, with his emphasis on Western
rationalism, saw a significant reduction in religion as a unifier of
the system: the secularization thesis. Jim recognizes this trend, but
he sees this largely as the failure of Christianity to confront the
challenge by clinging instead to a rigid set of religious symbolic
forms and functions.[14]

## Jim's Ethic

Weber constructed the historical development of ethical systems.
Jim, using earlier materials for his grounding,[15] develops an ethic.
It has a significant affinity with the ethic that Weber described as
existing in modern Western rationalization. He, like Weber, recognizes a secular as well as a religious ethic, but unlike Weber, he
retains a religious ethic in the now, rejecting the erosion of it into
a secular one.

Three questions arise: (1) How is Jim's ethic like Weber's model?
(2) How does Jim retain his religious orientation? (3) How is Jim's
ethic different from Weber's projection?

Throughout the two volumes, Jim repeatedly charges the person,
the community, and the society with *responsibility to make ethical
decisions*.[16] In the first volume he writes:

We can assess the accuracy and the adequacy of our knowledge and understanding of that to which we are responding. We can make judgments
about the significance of what evokes responses in the light of the seriousness of consequences and the effectiveness of means of action.... We
can investigate, test our findings, and make judgments.... [17] The theology
proposed in this book does not eliminate moral rules and principles, but
it does require a strong sense of the need for them to be general rules
whose application must be addressed to changing historical conditions....
Our understanding of what is morally required is not infallible, and it
develops historically in relation to events, and to forms of knowledge....
[R]ules and principles have to be open to revision and extension in the
light of alterations in natural, social, historical, cultural, and individual
conditions.[18]

In his profile of a theocentric ethic in the second volume, especially in the fifth feature of it, but also in the sixth and seventh, Jim reaffirms his ethic of responsibility:

The human venture is participation. Agents are participating not only in "transactions" with the immediate "recipients" of their initiatives; they are participants in the larger sphere of interaction, and even in the development of the natural world. . . . Thus to be a participant is to claim far more for human capacities of self determination, and the determination of courses of events and states of affairs. . . . The interpenetration of individuals and communities as *interacting* and *participating* within the context of the larger whole is not the only significant feature of a reconsideration of the relationship of parts to wholes. It follows . . . that the determination of right relationships between entities and the proper ends of human participation must take into account larger wholes of which individual entities are a part.[19]

For Jim, the job of ethicist is to enable others to make morally responsible choices by broadening and deepening their capacities for decision-making. It is not to provide a set of rules.[20]

As Schluchter points out, Weber did not explicitly develop the methodology for arriving at an ethic of responsibility, the reflexive principle. Jim does. His usual term for it is the process of "discernment."[21] To discern "involves discrimination, a keenness of perception, subtlety, and imagination . . . judgments about what is of greatest importance in understanding the life of the subject." The discerner brings his self, his experiences, interests, but most important his analytical skills, yet always with a perspective that is a reflection of his values. "But moral discernment does not flow with an automatic ease and pleasure. . . . Moral discernment is reflective; it is a rational activity."[22] Ethical questions arise when there is uncertainty, when our everyday responses are challenged.

Weber describes modern rationalized Western society as one in which the individual becomes isolated and depersonalized. The very high value placed on the individual and his rights leads to the judgment of things from the perspective of the individual, losing the social support of others, the communal judgment. But as Jim correctly perceives, to discern from this position is to have tunnel vision; discernment is both individual *and social*. But Jim warns, moral communities also have tunnel vision: "The purpose of moral discourse in communities is not in most cases to come to a unanimous conclusion. . . . It is to help form the 'consciences' of persons, to educate their rational activity, to enable them to think more clearly and thoroughly about the moral dimensions of aspects of life in the world."[23]

What we have said about an ethic of responsibility and its reflexive principle can apply to either a religious or a secular ethic. In the latter, a heavy burden is placed on the individual, a burden Weber saw as too great for most people—thus his pessimism.[24] The ethic of responsibility is basically rational-legal and seems to deny that there is any ethic of conviction of its support. For Jim, the nature of human nature is a part of the ordering of God, who is the source for conviction, if only we recognize our natural piety and respond to the "powers that sustain us and bear down on us, to the Ultimate Power on which all life depends."[25]

Thus Jim builds an ethic of conviction as infrastructure for his ethic of responsibility. Here he diverges sharply from Weber's analysis of our ethical state, coming "closer to the classic type of teleological ethics; values and ends are chosen and conditions needed to achieve or approximate them are developed. But there are boundaries within which particular ends ought to be pursued."[26] And he reminds us that religious communities are able to develop moral discourse, are apt to make strong moral judgments, and are under special obligation to develop an ethic of responsibility based on reflexive principles to assure sound moral judgments.[27]

## OVERVIEW AND COMMENTARY

Weber wrote as a social scientist who sought to show the development of modern Western society. He found the key to this in the rise of Western rationalism. The development of this rationality was not a simple unilinear cognitive process. It was the result of the complex interaction of meaningful human action, some of which was crystallized in social institutions within which were the seeds of change in themselves as autonomous units, yet interactive with one another, not always being "rational" in their relationships. I have found the analogy of bed springs to be the most immediately graspable expression of his understanding of historical development. His is a convincing explanation in general, but one that is subject to revision within his own methodology. Religion and religions were a central or near central element in all this, but especially reformation Christianity for the West. The rationale of his development led to what we now refer to as the theory of secularization, which rightly or wrongly is attributed to him. At the present time this theory is undergoing revision, with arguments that there are limits to the process,[28] which might be construed as indirect support for Jim's position.

Jim writes as a religious ethicist. His focus is on how to be a responsible this-worldly asceticist under present circumstances. His perception of the world we live in is that while it is significantly like that which Weber predicted, it is not fully so. He has the advantage of the years that have passed since Weber's writing and the increased knowledge and perspectivity of the social sciences that have since accrued. Putting it strongly, Jim is a social scientist who, from a deep abiding piety before God, has taken on as his life work the problem of *oughtness*—how to arrive at it, how to sustain ourselves in it. As a religious ethicist, Jim is fully aware of the effects of secularization, but he rejects the claim that the process is inevitable and terminal.

Another important difference between Weber and Jim is the way each assesses the place of dualism in Christianity. Weber accepts as a given the separation of this world from an "other" world—what is often referred to as the Lutheran *problemstellung*. Jim, again with the passage of time and new scholarship in theology—part of which is a reexamination of ante-Reformation doctrine—reduces significantly, if not closes entirely, that gap.

Weber's construction of the development of ethics tends to dismiss the ethic of conviction for the modern world. A lonely ethic of responsibility, based on reflexive principles, is what he saw developing in affinity with the "modernization" of the sociocultural system. It is a difficult ethic, probably unattainable for many.

Jim accepts the ethic of responsibility. He recognizes the difficulty, the ambiguities in which we become enmeshed when we seek to practice it. He recognizes, with Weber, the weakness of the individual and of the society in establishing such an ethical system. Unlike Weber, he retains an ethic of conviction—not like those described by Weber, but one based on the single principle that God exists and acts in this world, *one* pattern of which is in human actions. The corollary of this is that we, in piety, respond to God's acts to the best of our finite abilities. It is a tough act. It is so because the conviction is so specific, yet so universal, and as such we receive no particular proscriptions or prescriptions; that which makes life simpler for us also sets up alienative forces within us.

Moving closer to the persons—always dangerous for its tendency to imply motives, but in some ways most interesting: What of Weber and Jim? We know that Weber grew up in a family with a father uninterested in Christianity and a pietistic mother who came from a family deeply involved in the church, but with a strong unitarian bent. We know, too, that he was deeply attracted to his mother's family and spent time with them.[29] These influences were deep, but they may have been more of an inoculation than a feeding. Weber termed himself "unmusical" in religious matters. Certainly he did not mean that he rejected the significance of religions to sociocultural systems. His position as one of the most perceptive scholars of religion belies this. In Jim's terminology what he meant was that he had lost the link of piety to God. He had no convictional source for the ethic of responsibility he felt so strongly, and recognizing the limits of humankind, his response was pessimism, the "disenchantment of the world," life as limited to a "mechanical housing" or "iron cage" by modern impersonality.

Jim was brought up in a family in which his father was a pastor in a denomination that was a spin-off from the Lutheran State Church of Sweden—a result of the same pietistic movement that had occurred in Germany. Our home was one where our father was non-legalistically pietistic, our mother more so. Care brought forth fruit. Jim remained religiously musical. Thus when he reaches the position that the only meaningful ethic is an ethic of responsibility based on reflexive principles—as difficult as it is—he has a source of conviction that allows him some hope, some optimism in this world.

He chose from Milton words to mark the importance of the source of his conviction:

> So little knows
> Any, but God alone, to value right
> The good before him.... [30]

He affirms:

> God will not be manipulated
> God will not be ignored or denied
> God will be God[31]

# 6. Ethics and the Image of the Self in the Theology of Story

## L. Shannon Jung

And Isaac said to his father, Abraham, "My father!" And he said, "Here am I, my son." He said, "Behold the fire and the wood; but where is the lamb for a burnt offering?" (Genesis 22: 7).

An old story, told and retold, it continues to erupt in the imagination. It is also a good story. Why? I take a clue from Hans Frei's criterion that in a realistic narrative the characters "are firmly and significantly set in the context of the external environment, natural but more particularly social."[1] A good story is realistic. It is made credible by its location in a particular natural and social environment.

A good story goes beyond credibility, however. If it is to last— to be told and retold—it must also engage our imagination. The story conveys meaning in a way that is inseparable from its form. "Stories are not just a literary genre, therefore, but a form of understanding that is indispensable."[2] They become a part of what James Hillman calls our "soul history" rather than remaining "case history" or the recitation of events. A good story calls for a response, a new understanding, a reshaping.

These two characteristics of a "good story" can also be seen as appropriate to the work of ethics, which has the task of addressing the actual human situation with an engaging vision of the good. It has a stake in employing a realistic description of experiential reality, and also in maintaining the integrity and compellingness of the theological vision. Like a good story, good ethics must be realistic and engaging. Its mandate requires both a realistic assessment of human existence and an evaluative standard.

One of the central components of any story and any ethics is its conception of who human beings are, what forces affect them, how they struggle, what their limits are, why they act as they do. Without a realistic image of the self, both stories and ethics are doomed to fall on deaf ears.

Ethics, therefore, seeks to formulate a model of the self which describes life in society accurately. At the same time, Christian ethics must remain open to the insights of Christian theology or it will find itself without a vision of the good and, consequently, without an evaluative standard.

What I'm saying boils down to this: If a story is not realistic, it will be found incredible—interesting and engaging perhaps, but not to be taken seriously. If ethics does not adopt a realistic image of the self, it will be found irrelevant—a fascinating discipline or anthropological subject, but not to be seen as personally meaningful. If a story is not engaging, its realism does not matter. If ethics does not present a compelling vision, its descriptive accuracy counts for little. A realistic description of the self and an engaging vision of human possibility must go together; without both, the task of ethics is left undone.

I'm interested here in testing the image of the self that has been adopted by the theology of story. As a sociologist, I want to see if that image does indeed offer a realistic description of human existence. As a Christian ethicist, I want to see if the theology of story remains open to the engaging vision of human possibilities presented by the Christian faith.

This is an important task for two reasons. First, ethics has often been understood as simply a subsection of theology, without the recognition that ethics is particularly responsible for incorporating an accurate description of human existence. Second, ethics has sometimes been understood as only an analytical discipline with no attention to its persuasive force. Realistic description was seen as all that was needed; no attention was directed toward its engaging power.

To test the image of the self incorporated in the theology of story, I will begin by suggesting certain indispensable components of any theological image of the self. These components are attempts to spell out what is involved in descriptive realism *and* openness to the theological vision. These indispensable components will then be used as criteria and applied to the image of the self that is found in the theology of story. The essay will conclude with an evaluation of the liabilities and benefits of the theology of story.

The assumption behind this essay is that an ethics which builds upon a sociologically realistic description of the self has the potential to be more persuasive, more engaging, than one which does not. It is, therefore, vital that one's theological view of human nature be grounded in the most accurate understanding of human experience that is available. If this can be done while remaining open to a religious view of humankind, other benefits will emerge from such a grounding.

## INDISPENSABLE COMPONENTS OF THE SELF

1. The theological image of the self, to be realistic, must recognize that human life is conditioned by physical, psychological, and social factors. The self is located in a social matrix. The elucidation of this conditionedness is the forte of the social sciences. Ethicists who have ignored this aspect may tend to exaggerate either the transcendent freedom of human beings, e.g., the ethics of Karl Barth, or the human capacity for rational calculation in decision-making, e.g., the situation ethics of Joseph Fletcher.

2. The image must also take account of social structural influences on the self rather than simply more interpersonal, social psychological ones. The church member or student is influenced not only by the minister or teacher, but also by the structure of the church or educational institution. Influenced by its attachment to several communities, the self is not free to choose how those communities will shape its life to the same degree that it can shape its interpersonal relationships. Human activities are communal in nature; sociologically it is impossible to ignore the radical influence of social structures.

One danger here is that an image that fails to recognize such influences allows them to emerge without resistance. The ethics of Helmut Thielicke leans in this direction. Another danger is that the scope of ethics may be reduced to personal morality rather than include issues of social morality. Systems based on transactional analysis could reduce ethics to a matter of personal action or "adjustment."

3. The image must recognize social influences in a way that is consistent with, not contradictory to, the religious or moral characteristics of the self. Human experience is not two-tiered. It is through social interaction and personal directedness that the self experiences and expresses its religious and moral character. Human beings experience the unity of the self in everyday life. Our friends and others communicate the forgiveness of God to us, for example; that forgiveness does not come *ex vacuo*.

Without the integration of both aspects of the self, the ethicist finds himself with two unrelated images—the social self of *Historie* and the intentional, transcendent self of *Geschichte*. The ethics of Reinhold Niebuhr, despite his efforts to the contrary, tends to promote this bifurcation. Ultimately this might result in the assertion that religious morality has little to do with social life.[3]

These three components specify what is entailed in an adequate description of the empirical self for theological ethics. They suggest certain indispensable qualities that must be exhibited by any image of the self—what the human being "is." Ethics, however, is also concerned with the relation of the "ought" to the "is," the ideal to the actual. It is not content with conformity to social norms but proceeds with a theologically informed conception of the "ought." Thus, in correspondence with the descriptive standards, there are also certain components of theological openness that an image must exhibit. The theological image of the self goes beyond the sociological, and must do so if it is to serve as a model for ethics. These qualities indicate the self's capacity to become engaged and are indispensable to theological openness.

1. The image must recognize the fact that the self is purposeful, and is not simply conditioned by external forces. It is essential that the element of intentional freedom in human life not be reduced to an "oversocialized" conception of the self.[4] Without this element of intentionality any talk of moral responsibility is absurd.

2. The image of the self must incorporate a concern for questions of internal meaning rather than simply of external behavior. All of us realize that we are able to experience meaning. This enables us to measure external behavior according to an internal standard of meaning. What one person finds to be a highly evocative sculpture may leave another person cold, for example, or what one person

interprets as an act of kindness may appear to be condescending to another.

It is through internal meaning and imagination that we evaluate the past, interpret the present, and project future possibilities. This internal capacity enables us to make sense of external events; thus it is important to indicate the internal ability of the self to interact with its environment.

3. A theologically adequate image of the self must remain open to the irrational, the indeterminate, and the mysterious in human experience. An ethics which adopts so empirical and quantitative an image of the self that it drives out ambiguity and transcendence has ceased to reckon with lived experience. It has substituted its own creation for the living world. Human behavior cannot be translated into rigid models without reduction. Theological as well as sociological models can reduce human life to their own concerns and thereby lose the richness and mystery of human experience.

These two sets of indispensable components do not arise from a systematic integration of the relationships between theological and sociological images, nor is any claim being made regarding their comprehensiveness.[5] They are ingredients which *cannot be excluded* from an adequate image of the self.

## THE THEOLOGY AND ETHICS OF STORY

The theology and ethics of story as a theological approach is being tested here to determine if it incorporates illuminative power.[6] Since a central tenet in any theology is its doctrine of human nature, judgments concerning the theology of story will be based, to some extent, on the adequacy of the image of the self which it promotes— its realism *and* its conduciveness to theological communication. Several claims being made for the theology of story suggest that it is well worth such an assessment.

Stephen Crites offers the strongest commendation of the theology of story. He speaks of the "narrative quality of experience": accordingly, his central thesis is that human experience *is* an incipient narrative. Our consciousness mediates between "sacred" and "mundane" stories, which in turn "give qualitative substance to the form of experience because it is itself an incipient story."[7] The suggestion is that theology would be well served to adopt a form that reflects the form of human experience. Stories exhibit this resonance. He furthermore argues that narrative has the capacity to unite experience and thought; theory and practice are shown to be integrated in story. Stories reveal the split between thought and feeling (mind and body) to be artificial.

Sallie TeSelle offers a similar advantage of the theology of story in her book *Speaking in Parables*. She claims that parables, stories, and poems have the ability to communicate the word of God in our time. Theology that is "overly abstract, conceptual, and systemic... separates thought and life, belief and practice...,making it more difficult if not impossible for us to believe in our hearts what we confess with our lips."[8] In contrast, the theology of story remains concrete, experiential, and confessional; thus it serves the hearing of the gospel by uniting language, belief, and community.

Another way of making the points that Crites and TeSelle do might be the recognition that the theology of story can join affection and reflection. Both theology and ethics cry out for this union. The self does not first get its theological doctrines "right" and then adopt an embodied worldview. Nor does the self begin with the choice of certain norms and virtues and mold its decisions and dispositions in those directions. We do not necessarily determine what "is" (theologically or otherwise) and then move to what we "ought" to do.[9] Those who attempt these forms of theologizing feel the frustration of having somehow to bridge the chasm between reflection and practice. We first respond to stories and live in the light of those stories we find significant. To be sure, different stories and creative metaphors can lead us to reflect on the truth of the story we are living. Living only on the basis of our feelings can be as debilitating as living only on the basis of our thoughts. The theology of story evokes emotional response in a way that lends itself to union with reflection.

Our affections are somehow "touched" by stories, and that is why a good story moves us—we "feel it in our bones" and respond viscerally. The theology of story is the kind of religious and ethical reflection that embodies the experience about which it is reflecting. The mode of reflection fits the experience it seeks to communicate.[10]

## EMPIRICAL SELF AND STORY

Does the image of self contained in the theology of story exhibit the indispensable components outlined earlier?

1. The image must recognize human conditionedness. One characteristic of the image set forth by these theologians, and also by sociologists, is that human experience is always particular and limited. The focus of this image is not on the universal qualities of human experience, but rather on the definite and concrete experience of the person in his or her own history. People are always limited by their finitude, a finitude that includes physical embodiment, historical location, and social conditionedness.

In the story of Abraham's journey to sacrifice his son, Isaac's question, "Where is the lamb for a burnt offering?" clearly implies the historical and social conditions within which he and his father lived.

The recognition of human limitation becomes particularly important for ethicists who view the theology of story as a promising orientation for their work. They understand that ethics itself is always formulated from within a particular social location. Indeed, it cannot escape that limit. The theologian of story is aware that the contemporary bias toward self-determination is itself a result of human limitation and social conditionedness. There is no position that could free the moral agent from the limitations of time, place, and circumstance: We are particular human beings who act within a particular social context. This emphasis has obvious affinities with sociology in general, and the sociology of knowledge in particular. It likewise implies that ethics may have to recognize that the only universal moral judgments are formal, and cannot be invariably applied. Rather than bemoan the impossibility of formulating an eternal code of morality, ethics will have "to learn to attend afresh to the way of life of particular communities and particular men, though without sacrificing its yearning for universalizability."[11]

2. The image must recognize the influence of social structures as well as interpersonal relationships. A second, related characteristic of the image of the self set forth by some theologians of story is that human experience is limited by the wider social context and is relative to the historical conditions of social structures.

Three aspects of the story of Abraham's temptation indicate that the narrator has firmly placed it within the social structure of the Israelite religion. When Abraham wants to be alone with his son, he tells his servants that they intend to go onto a mountain to pray, a customary practice at that time on journeys. The narrator also mentions several details about the nature of sacrificial offerings—how the altar is built, Abraham's carrying the torch and the knife, his laying the wood "in order." Third, the whole institution of sacrifice and the cult within which it is set can be intuited from Isaac's question and from the provision of the ram for a burnt offering.[12]

The fact that the biblical writer has set this story within a socio-structural, as well as an interpersonal, context does not, of course, mean that all theologians of story share this element of the image. Yet this characteristic is essential for both theological and socio-logical reasons. Theologically, any view of human nature which does not take into account the influence of social structures runs the dangers of privatization and of lapsing into complete subjec-tivity. Any story could be considered just as valid as any other, since there could be no appeal to historical standards of evaluation. Furthermore, there could be no sense of community based on a shared story. Without the recognition of social structures, theolog-ical images run the risk of subjectivity: Whatever is emotionally appealing becomes the touchstone by which stories are accepted or rejected. To avoid this, the image needs the balance provided by awareness of the external givenness of structures.

The sociological danger involves a failure to recognize the influ-ence of structures and a lapse into psychology. Certainly the achieve-ments of sociology are persuasive enough to negate any image of the self which does not include as an integral feature the social nature of human knowledge and action.

One gets a sense of the importance of these "wider stories" for the constitution of the self from Stephen Crites's assertion that some stories may lie so deep in our consciousness that they have in fact formed that consciousness [13] Those structures have become a part of us. Other theologians of story similarly emphasize the influence of the social world, either by explicit mention of social structures or—with Crites—of the way these stories and structures have be-come internalized. It nevertheless appears to me that the category "story" is sufficiently vulnerable to privatization that care must be taken not to restrict the meaning of social influence to social psychological elements only, rather than to include structural components as well. This appears to be the greatest hazard of the image of self contained in the theology of story.

3. The image must integrate social, everyday experience with religious or moral experience. A third characteristic expressed by theologians of story is that human life is experiential, that life is unified through experience. This anthropological accent calls into question those theologies which separate "natural" from "religious" aspects of life. Narrative theology is particularly well suited to express this unity.

Notice, for example, how smoothly the Abraham story integrates the concrete fact of the journey to Moriah with the instructions of the angel of the Lord. Abraham experiences the everyday as religious and the religious as continuous with human experience.

The unity of experience uncovers the artificiality of systems of ethics which incorporate a view of humans as rationally calculating courses of action from the vantage point of disinterestedness. Our moral notions, Stanley Hauerwas asserts, "are not the product of abstract reasoning," but rather "arise from the needs and interests and demands embedded in our lives together."[14] Through the category "story" the relationship between religion and morality is shown to be grounded in the same experiential base. We are formed mainly by those metaphors and stories gained from experience which have become embodied in our intentions. Obviously these theologians share a concern for the centrality of human experience with sociologists. Unlike the sociologists, however, these theologians would not limit their understanding of experience to external or behavioral manifestations.

There are several implications of the adoption of this image of the self for doing Christian ethics. The image focuses on everyday processes. This suggests the need for a renewed interest in moral character, an ethics which recognizes the everyday process of moral development. Once the understanding of the moral life is expanded beyond decision-making, Christian ethicists can begin to understand that ethics also involves an orientation or disposition toward the world. This enables the ethicist to integrate vision, or guiding metaphors, with morality. It also facilitates the understanding of life as a process of growing, developing, *and* making decisions in the

everyday world. The fact that ethics has attended so dispropor-
tionately to decision-making may explain why insufficient energy
has been directed toward the development of an adequate foundational anthropology.[15]

Though the theologians of story have paid little explicit attention
to sociology, their mode of theological reflection is compatible with
modern sociological theory. They recognize the conditioned nature
of human life. Some do include the influence of social-structural
arrangements as well as interpersonal influences, though I suspect
still more attention needs to be paid to structural factors. Furthermore, they find in human experience a way to integrate the social
and the religious-moral aspects of human life. In this way they can
speak of the unity of plot, theme, guiding metaphor, or character.
Finally, with their focus on everyday routinization they reveal an
affinity with sociological generalization. Thus the theology of story
can be helpful to the Christian ethicist, who is called to integrate
theological affirmations and sociological analysis.

One caveat must be entered here. Ted Estess reminds us that the
motif "story" is also finally a model, an abstraction which—though
it may be close to lived experience—can obscure certain aspects of
lived experience. Life may be an "inenarrable contraption": "Story"
as a category "may obscure those chaotic and disordered experiences which are part of human life."[16] It may hide the many life
experiences that do seem purposeless. Certainly not all life can be
seen as directed by purposive action. Some things simply happen.
Estess likewise reminds us that sometimes we are unable to see how
momentary experiences are connected. We don't always enjoy a
comprehensive view of our lives.[17] Narrative theology may be
tempted to lose a sense of the absurdity of life and of temporal and
spatial limitations. The value of these caveats lies in their refusal
to allow us to see life stories as linear and unambiguous. They also
warn us not to identify the model of story with human life.

## THEOLOGICAL OPENNESS AND THE SELF

I have thus far enunciated assumptions about the self which seem
to be shared by theologians of story and sociologists; however,
theologians of story make certain assumptions which go beyond

standard sociological limits, a consideration of which may be informative to sociology as well as ethics.

1. The image must recognize that the self is intentional as well as conditioned. Theologians of story are sensitive to the conditioning limitations of the self; at the same time, they are concerned that the intentional nature of the self not be obscured by the legitimate importance of physical and social influences. Persons do not simply absorb and live out the social conditions which affect them; rather, they interpret, choose, and act on the basis of their intentions. Human beings act through their environment and limitations to shape their lives. They are not simply determined creatures who are acted upon. They are also moral agents. They live out their intentions within the range of and *through* their physical and social limitations.

The opening verse of the Abraham story certainly exhibits this intentional feature. It notes that "God tested Abraham" and implies that Abraham was free to obey God's demand or ignore it. The story can thus be understood as a test of obedience.

The ethicist who views "story" as a resource for describing the moral life focuses on the nature of character. The category of "moral character" indicates the connection between a person's intentions and actions: One's character is formed by, and forms, his or her intentions and actions. The image being expressed is that persons are self-determining but are also shaped by their choices, which are themselves conditioned by the social context; this image therefore meets the first criterion of theological integrity—the human capacity for intentionality, without exaggerating the range of self-determination.

2. The image must indicate the place of internal meaning. The category "story" also indicates a quality of commitment or engagement. As James Wiggins puts it, "A story of real importance is not an argument so much as it is a presentation and an invitation. It . . . invites participation in imaginative responses to reality."[18] Likewise, TeSelle speaks of the parables of Jesus as "calls to decision," concerned with "what we are in the process of believing, knowing, and becoming *in our lives*."[19] There is a process of becoming engaged and committed to a metaphor or story which directs our intentionality and molds our character. To be theologically

adequate, an image of the self must recognize the internal capacity to find meaning, to become engaged.

A linked characteristic of the image of the self conveyed by the theology of story focuses on internal meaning rather than simply on external behavior. James Hillman's distinction between "case history" (a biography of historical events) and "soul history" (the history of internal meaning), mentioned earlier, is instructive here. He writes that "without the sense of soul, we have no sense of history. We never enter it. This core of soul that weaves events together into the meaningful patterns of tales and stories recounted by reminiscing creates history. History is story first and fact later."[20] Stories are particularly well suited to express the interdependence of internal meaning and external history. "Symbol, metaphor, image in incarnated speech and action must be cherished and honored as a medium for such expression, and these occur most frequently— though not exclusively—in stories."[21]

The chronicler of the Abraham story has left implicit much of the internal struggle which the patriarch must have felt. The story of Job, for example, offers a much more explicit look into this character's soul. Nevertheless, there are some touches which suggest that Abraham was not unfeelingly obedient. He carries the torch and the knife himself, rather than ask Isaac to do that. The narrator twice mentions that "they went both of them together." When Isaac asks where the lamb is, his father tells him that "God will provide himself the lamb for a burnt offering, my son." Whether or not he believed that, Abraham clearly wanted to spare his son the pain of knowing what was about to happen. Perhaps the narrator does not explicitly mention Abraham's feelings because he wants to convey the important internal meaning that Abraham had decided God's command ought to be obeyed, no matter what the price. Finally, of course, the story is open to interpretation by the reader or hearer.

Through their tendency to describe only external action, many sociologists—reflecting the contemporary worldview as much as analyzing it—have participated in reductionism.[22] They have restricted consideration of the internal life of meaning and motivation—an aspect of the self which becomes very significant for an ethics of character, and indeed for any ethics which recognizes moral development and the virtues. Since the relationship between the internal and external aspects of the self is significant for analysts of the moral life, the integration of the two through the categories of "story" and "character" commends itself to ethical investigation.

The precociousness and looseness of this theological style does, however, suggest the importance of careful analysis in further delineating the structures of human experience and their interaction with symbolic meaning. These two characteristics of the image—the self's ability to become engaged and attention to the internal life of the self—indicate that the theology of story has met the second criterion of theological openness: a concern for questions of internal meaning.

3. The image must remain open to the indeterminate and the mysterious in life. Another characteristic of the self found in narrative theology is that human experience transcends the expected, the quantifiable, and the empirical. Indeed, it is often the *unexpected* in stories (our own or others') that jolts us out of a one-dimensional world and makes us recognize that life is not simply objective. Theologically we cannot accept a criterion that is limited to quantifiable verification. To do so would be to deny the life of the spirit, the possibility of belief, and our identity as moral agents.

One fascinating quality of the Abraham story is that we imagine how Abraham felt, expecting that his only son would indeed die on that altar. Then the unexpected happens: Isaac is spared. A twist occurs in the story, and though we knew how *that* story would end, we rejoice with Abraham in the providence of God.

The story has an integrity of its own. It cannot be reduced or dissolved conceptually. It can deliver us from our all-too-human expectations and from the tyranny of our own thoughts.[23] It can open our eyes to the mysterious, to the inbreaking power of the new. Stories can help us reimagine our own lives. They can express the ambiguity, the self-transcendence, and the numinous that scientific and rational consciousness so often ignores. Thus, theology of story meets the third criterion of openness: the possibility of experiencing the unexpected and transrational.

## CONCLUSIONS

This analysis indicates that the theology of story incorporates an image of the self that recognizes the intentionality of the self, the place of internal meaning, and remains open to the indeterminate and mysterious in human experience. Since this image exhibits the indispensable components of both descriptive realism and theological openness, theology of story seems worthy of further attention and refinement.

Attention needs to be paid, first, to clarifying the external social structures of experience and to the relationship between experience and symbolic meaning.[24] Without that, the legitimate insights of sociology might be dismissed, and the theology of story could become lost in the subjectivity of experience, i.e., the trap of any-story-is-just-as-good-as-any-other The "looseness" of the theology of story could lend itself to the privatization of myth or the failure to recognize phenomenological limits. This would be a dangerous, if not debilitating, shortcoming for the theology of story.

On the other hand, there are several benefits which the theology of story has to offer. The first is motivational. Because a good story engages us and calls for our response, it is able to join feeling and thinking. We recognize ourselves in the story. It addresses us totally rather than appealing to our cognitive and emotional faculties separately. Talk of motivating people and the split between reflection and affection are transcended in hearing the story. We are addressed by the irreducible particular in the story. Rather than devising some strategy to summon belief or haranguing about doctrinal differences, the story invites us to live out its truth. As Hauerwas puts it, "The gospel is a story that gives you a way of being in the world," that involves "the agent in a way of life."[25] The personal motivation which the story evokes, which may be the most authentic mode of persuasion, overcomes the split between reflection and affection. The individual person becomes committed to a story and makes it part of his or her *soul*.

A related benefit of stories is that they offer both self-understanding and the understanding of others. With the aid of a story, human beings can tie their experiences together and give a degree of cohesion and intelligibility to their lives. Stories help us make sense of our lives. The best stories are those that help us understand the interrelation of our particular joys, struggles, disappointments, hopes, and anxieties. Thus there may be a "natural law of narrative," a phenomenological "fit" between our attempts to understand our lives and the story. Stories enable us to forge a way through perplexities and realize the implications of our commitments.

They may also guide us toward changing those aspects of our lives with which we are dissatisfied and make our visions more inclusive. We may let our own stories come into contact with those of other people. Indeed, it is through others' stories that we may better come to understand them. Stories also enable us to understand our limits, which are also our enablements. Rather than simply being shaped by the world, however, our stories also shape the world: The world changes with our interpretation of it. Thus, we can reimagine and be reshaped within our limits. By "restorying" our lives, we are able to break old patterns. Indeed, psychiatric therapy has been interpreted as the effort to help individuals reimagine and change lifestyles that have become destructive—to tell new stories.[26]

A third benefit relates to the two anthropological assumptions made in this essay: that human beings are limited and that they are free within those limits. Reflected in the two sets of indispensable components is my belief that human beings are existentially bound to address both dimensions: the self as he or she is and the self as possibility—the "is" and the "ought" or "could be." There are structures which constrain us and possibilities which beckon us within those defining structures. The story reminds us that we are concrete and particular beings at the same time that it provides entry into those myths that suggest what we could be. It is because a story can bridge the gap between the concrete and the mysterious, the everyday and the envisioned, that it can relate the theological-ethical vision to the everyday world. It can help traverse the distance between what is and what ought to be, between sociology and ethics—practical moral reasoning.

# Part III. THE SOCIOLOGY OF FAITH

# 7. On Freedom, Love, and Community

## George A. Hillery, Jr.

The interplay of one's values and research is a topic more often talked about than demonstrated. The research to be discussed here is an example of such interplay. All research reflects the researcher's values, but in some instances the relationship is more obvious than in others. In the present case, the values guiding the research stemmed equally from a desire to solve a sociological problem concerning the nature of community and from a personal commitment to Jesus Christ. I do not apologize for either my science or my religion. Whatever is accomplished in each area must stand on its own merits. I wish to show the unfolding of a particular line of research as it has developed from scientific to other-than-scientific areas and back to science again (though the process cannot be delineated that sharply).

Of all fields of sociology, the study of community is one of the most basic to understanding the manner in which Christian groups can be adequately constituted. As a Christian, I have discovered some things of vital importance to my life, on which my science has never touched more than fleetingly. Foremost among these is love. In studying both community and love, it has become apparent that one of the basic contexts, even mechanisms, in which these phenomena operate is freedom. To gain an adequate comprehension of these things, I have found that I needed both science and religion. It is the interplay of these systems that I want to discuss.

A theory is composed of many parts. There is the set of propositions showing the relation between variables in a formal sense. There are also the definitions of the variables. As important as any portion of the theory are the assumptions on which it is based, particularly the assumption concerning the types of truths employed. In science this assumption is unstated because everyone is aware that only one type of truth is being employed—scientific truth, or truth based on data determined by objective presentation of physical evidence.

In his monumental study of social change, Pitirim Sorokin postulated other kinds of truth. In addition to science ("sensate" truth), there is truth based on faith ("ideational" truth). He went on to propose a third type, one which integrated both of the others: integralist truth. This article will take Sorokin's ideas as a point of departure and attempt to demonstrate the necessity of employing more than one type of truth in the study of social action.[1]

## TYPES OF TRUTH

The problem of exploring the nature of truth is both metaphysical and epistemological. The metaphysical problem involves the nature of the assumptions concerning reality. The scientist assumes that reality is based on physical data, whereas a mystic assumes further that there is a superphysical—i.e., a spiritual—reality. Regardless of one's assumptions about reality, there are different ways of experiencing or knowing that reality, in the sense of the type of evidence one will accept as truth. The experience may be direct, such as hearing sounds, being inebriated, or (in the experience of some to be studied here) perceiving God. This is the experiential aspect. Such experience can only partly (if at all) be communicated to others. Some types of knowledge may be communicated precisely, such as the designation of sounds by means of musical notes, determining the alcoholic content of blood, or describing the fact that Christians believe in a trinitarian God. This is the objective aspect.

The combination of the metaphysical and epistemological dimensions reveals four types of truths (no claim is made that these are the only types of truths): mystical, theological, sensory, and scientific. Most written discussions are objective, whether scientific or theological, in the sense in which *objective* is being used here. Seldom can writing be fully experiential, though poetry comes close, as do novels. This essay will concern itself mainly with *indicating* experiential truths. It cannot duplicate them. In contrast, there is frequently a dependence of objective on experiential truth. Scientists will tend to be more satisfied when they have done an experiment themselves. The writing of theologians has been known to change drastically upon their undergoing a mystical experience, but the separation between the two truths is often quite discrete. An example from sensory truth will help show the distinction: One who has never been drunk may do a breath analysis and establish that someone else is drunk. He may understand this analysis sufficiently to cause the drunk to be placed in jail, but he will not experientially understand what it is to be drunk. The same can be said for mystical truth. The theologian may understand that Christians believe in a trinitarian God. He may himself have faith in such a God, and may even be able to prescribe certain theological readings to help someone else see his point, but this does not mean that he has "known" God in the sense of having had a mystical experience.

My discussion will be based on all four types of truths. Special emphasis is placed on the relation between mystical, sensory, and scientific truth. The experiential pole of the epistemological dimension was made possible through participant observation. The objective pole was reached mainly through questionnaires. One of the major purposes in presenting such a discussion is to help demarcate more precisely the boundaries of science. A major assumption of this essay is that the world cannot be understood purely from the scientific point of view. The question then arises: What is the perspective that exists outside of science? Granted that some of the topics to be treated here are not considered to be *sociology* as the term is generally used. However, the thesis being advanced is that in order to understand social action, to study society properly (i.e., socio*logy*), the customary horizons of sociology must be extended.

## THEORY OF ORGANIZATIONAL FREEDOM

Much of my sociological work has been devoted to the development of a theory of communal organizations, basic to which is a general taxonomy of human groups.[2] A major point of the taxonomy is that it depicts changes in human behavior: When degree of institutionalization is held constant, as between communal and formal organizations, then a change in whether a group gives primacy to a specific goal means that differences will also occur in the behavior of the members of the groups. From this reasoning, three hypotheses may be developed. These hypotheses are based on the observation of differences in behavior among groups as one moves across the theoretical boundary between communal and formal organizations. The latter here are defined as those groups which give primacy to specific goals. *Primacy* refers to the purpose for which a group is designed, apart from which it would have another meaning; *specific* refers to something measurable. Communal organizations, by contrast, are defined as groups which do not give primacy to specific goals.

1. If a group is primarily oriented to the attainment of a specific goal, it will exclude familial behavior—i.e., formal organizations exclude families.
2. The greater the deprivation of freedom among groups, the greater the antagonism of those deprived.
3. Only if a group is not primarily oriented to the attainment of a specific goal will it maximize the freedom of its members—i.e., communal organizations maximize freedom more than do formal organizations.

Data have been gathered that permit the testing of these hypotheses developed from my earlier work. The test is based on forty-six groups.[3] From this research, we may conclude in terms of this portion of the theory that: (1) deprivation of freedom is associated with violence in confined and non-staff groups of formal organizations (e.g., prison inmates); (2) members of communal organizations perceive themselves to be more free than members of formal organizations; and (3) there is little evidence that formal organizations exclude families, except for the lack of interaction across the staff-inmate split.

These findings indicate that the general classification of human groups has value in understanding why people behave as they do. Group structure appears to make some difference in human behavior.[4] But the theory relates only three variables: group goals, perceived freedom, and violence. The task now is to see if the meaning of this theory can be expanded, particularly by incorporating other types of truths. We will examine sensory, mystical, and theological truth. The data with which the discussion will be concerned revolve around the concept of love.

## IDEAL TYPES AS IDEALS

To pursue this analysis, the technique of the ideal type will be employed. Such a technique requires that one construct a model that is both pure and simplified. This model represents the conditions that would exist if all unnecessary things were removed, if all contradictory or contaminating influences were eliminated. It is akin to the idea of the frictionless surface or the absolute zero of the physicist, or (in a very crude sense) it is something like the germ-free mice that have been raised in certain laboratories. These are not necessarily or usually "reality," but by studying them, or as close as we can come to them, we learn something about reality. Normally, the purpose of constructing ideal types is not to depict a morally ideal situation—nor an immorally ideal one. However, since we are dealing with spiritual truth, such will be one of the aims here. The ideal types to be constructed will represent extreme moral poles.

I will build four ideal types: the family, the monastery, the business, and the prison. These types are to be developed in two stages. The first employs variables from the hypotheses examined in the previous section. Thus, ideal types of groups are to be built (1) for those with maximum and minimum freedom, and (2) for those that give primacy to specific goals and those that do not. In other words, the ideal types will vary along the organizational and the freedom dimensions. The second stage consists of using variables related to freedom and goal attainment but heretofore unexamined: love and personal involvement.

### The Family

We start with that relationship in which a man and a woman give of each other, to each other, as completely as possible. In this act, they raise to the highest point their freedom of choice and discipline. Each must become disciplined to the other, and in so doing, each has maximum access to the other, including, of course, freedom to the body of the other.[5]

Even these freedoms are not complete. For example, there is no group in which everyone can be the leader. Someone must lead, and thus one type of choice becomes closed to the one who does not lead. Second, because our bodies are discrete entities, we cannot give of ourselves completely, simply because we are separate. Ogden Nash has put it best: "We'd free the incarcerate race of man/That such a doom endures/Could only you unlock my skull,/Or I creep into yours."[6]

From this giving, children arise. This introduction of new persons into the two-person goup immediately limits freedom of choice: Children are not sexually accessible to parents or to each other. Freedom of discipline is also limited: Children cannot give to parents as much as parents can give to children or to each other. Finally, both freedoms become radically diminished or even terminated when children establish their own families.

As this relationahip is extended beyond the family to the village community (or even the city), freedoms are further limited. This limitation applies particularly to the general decrease of freedom in bodily contact. However, except for the reduction of this bodily freedom, community members in the ideal type still give of each other and receive from each other to the fullest, relative to other groups.[7]

### The Monastery

The monastery is built of community relationships (in the sense of village or city community) that are otherwise exclusive of the family. No family relationships occur in the monastery we are building here. There are two additional features: The most successful monasteries have been limited to one sex, and the members dedicate themselves to their God. Since community relationships in the monastery prevail only apart from the family, and since the group is unisexual, sexual giving to their God is irrelevant (at the very least). With this exception, the monk gives himself as completely as possible to his God and his God reciprocates, to the extent that the monk's humanity will permit. This second limitation is comparable to that of the spousal relationship: Complete giving (and receiving) is not possible because the monk is human.

In one sense, the monastery lacks some of the freedoms found in the family, especially bodily freedom, both sexual and parental. In another sense, the monks are more free, and here we must assume a spiritual reality: The monk gives and receives from his God without the complications arising from erotic relationships. In other words, the monk gives (disciplines) himself as completely as possible to his God and only to his God, and he is thus able to receive from his God in like manner. Although this freedom is necessary to understand the monastery, it cannot be understood on a scientific basis. We can say scientifically only that the monk believes this to be so and acts accordingly. From the viewpoint of scientific truth, the monastery has fewer freedoms than the family.

### The Business

All familial relations are excluded from the ideal typical business relation. The businessman is in this sense a monk, as Weber observed. Only those relations are permitted which are pertinent to the specific goal of the business. Regardless of whether the customer is a wife or a child, one customer is treated as any other: "Business is business." This means all other alternatives and all other disciplines are also removed. The freedoms are also accordingly reduced.

### The Prison

All significant choices are removed from a particular segment of this group, the inmates. Discipline in the ideal type is at its maximum, but it is not a discipline that arises from free choice; it is enforced. The goal is quite specific: custody of the inmates. Still, the goal is not that of the inmates but of the controlling staff. Because the goal is external to the inmates, and because individuals are discrete entities, discipline cannot be complete, if only because the prison in this type does not have access to men's minds.

### Types of Love

Up to this point, freedom has been examined only as it relates to discipline, but freedom requires more attention than this. The marital pair developed two possible freedoms: disciplined freedom (a freedom requiring sharing and sacrificing) and conditional freedom (in which one's freedom is limited—or conditioned—by other people or by external circumstances). The necessity of disciplined freedom is obvious, insofar as both partners give up the right to themselves. Conditional freedom arises because the freedom is tied to that of one other person. The monastery has only disciplined freedom. In the ideal sense, the monk's freedom is influenced only by his relation to his God, not by other people. The business has only conditional freedom—the sharing and sacrifice are not important in themselves but are only important as things the business must do. Similarly, the egoistic freedom (doing what one wishes to do) of the business is curtailed by the need for conditional freedom. In the ideal type of the prison, there are no freedoms at all.

These ideal types in turn suggest another set. The same groups are involved, only different variables are used. The variables here are relationships to persons and to society. In introducing these variables, we are also using experiential truth, especially in relation to personal relationships, since the two poles of this variable are love and indifference. A central premise of this discussion is that love cannot be understood unless it has been experienced.

Because of the nature of experiential truth, any verbal description is necessarily limited. We can *suggest* a definition and a typology of love, we cannot *give* one. Accordingly, love is that condition wherein one attempts to work for the best interests of the beloved. The word used by St. Paul and the earliest Christians to discuss love was *agapé*, which meant love (as here defined) in its purest sense—i.e., self-giving love. An alternative was *eros*, which has come to denote what Renaissance poets called "profane" love. The original meaning was not limited to sexual love, but we shall emphasize that meaning here.

Two other types of love are designated as friendship and affection, admitting that the terms are not completely adequate to describe either.[8] Friendship occurs between persons who may or may not be related to each other. Affection refers both to love of parents for children and vice versa, though the emphasis here is on parents' love. One could provide additional types, but these will do for our purposes. These types of love may be related to two variables: physical contact and detachment. Physical contact is essential to erotic and parental love but is not important to friendship or agapeic love. Parental love demands that the parent be willing to relinquish certain rights to the child; that is, the parent should exhibit some degree of detachment. Normally one does not consider such a condition necessary to erotic love.[9] There is a certain element of possessiveness to both friendship and erotic love. Agapeic love also carries a sense of detachment; indeed, it reveals the maximum amount of detachment love can have, if we consider Jesus as the prototype. I will emphasize the erotic and agapeic forms.

The other variable to be considered is one's relationship to society. The two poles of this variable are involvement and isolation. Involvement requires the maximum of interaction, isolation the least. Considering the relation of these variables to the four ideal-typical groups, in terms of the typology of love, it is apparent that erotic love and affection characterize the family, whereas friendship and agapeic love characterize the monastery.

The monastery may seem to be the most contradictory type of the four: How can one be in a loving relationship with others and yet be isolated? The solution lies in the concept of detached or agapeic love. The monk, being human, is not characterized only by *agapé*: Real friendships develop among the monks for each other; although this was officially discouraged in the past, it still happened. Nevertheless, the goal toward which the monk strives is detached love, which he can achieve in at least seven ways. Four of these are in terms of vows and commitments (those of the Trappist-Cistercian Order are being used): celibacy, obedience, poverty, and stability. The remaining expressions of detachment are implicitly contained in a vow of "conversion of life": asceticism, separation from the world, and the prayer of quiet.

Celibate love is a form of detached love. The purpose of this detachment is usually expressed in terms of the consequent ability to be open to a nonpossessive love for everyone. The detachment found in obedience is central to monastic—particularly Cistercian—life. The monk vows to live under the guidance of a rule and an abbot. The abbot is his temporal lord, the one who represents Christ to him. In offering obedience to the abbot, the monk does not give up his independence. He may leave whenever he wishes. But he does practice obedience as a form of humility. The same may be said of poverty, which again is a form of detachment, this time from the cares and seductions of the material world. The vow of stability detaches the monk from any temptation to leave the monastery to try to find his salvation elsewhere.

Asceticism is a form of detachment from the material world, but the relation to love may not be as apparent. The most immediate connection of asceticism with love can be seen in its further relationship to humility. The monk deprives himself of food, sleep, speech, and the like, first in obedience to his God, because of his love for his God. But there is a further dimension: In asceticism, the monk is saying in effect that he will leave to his God any provision of earthly or spiritual pleasures—he will seek none himself. Separation from the world is in itself a detachment from the world—the ultimate purpose is to permit the monk greater opportunity for undisturbed meditation and prayer—often, prayer for the world. The prayer of quiet is the most basic form of monastic prayer. It consists of a condition in which the monk thinks no thoughts, but simply stands in loving adoration, physically and mentally silent before his God. This prayer is the ultimate form of the monk's expression of love for his God, and it has been reported on occasion to be accompanied by an experience of union with God.

Detachment in monks is relatively easy to understand, if only because it is so pervasive in their lives. There is an element of detachment in erotic love as well, because no one can be completely accessible to another. There is an even more important aspect to detachment. The definition of love used here suggests that one works for the best interests of the beloved. If it is in the best interests of the beloved for the lover to leave, then failure to comply will mean less love on the part of the lover. If the spouse is ill, for example, and it would be better for the other partner to leave the spouse alone, then love itself will demand the degree of detachment that would permit the spouse the needed isolation. Thus erotic love cannot be completely possessive. Even in the very act of commitment, when one member totally commits oneself to the other, then to that extent one becomes detached from oneself. There is another who must be considered, even as one considers one's very own self.

Shifting to the other two ideal types, love is absent as far as the system is concerned in the prison and the business. The opposite of love here is not hate or conflict but indifference. One does not hate that toward which he is indifferent, but he may hate or even murder the one he loves, as statistics will attest. The businessman does not necessarily love his business, but must be involved with it. In prison's isolation, then, comes the ultimate negation of the basic values of community: love and involvement.

From this analysis of both businesses and prisons, it is apparent that formal organizations are antithetical to the basic value of love. Formal organizations are system processes used to get things done in the spirit of efficiency. The attempt to operate a community, a marriage, or a monastery along business lines is essentially immoral, since such a course of action denies the very moral basis on which the existence of communal organizations is predicated. For example, if one were to make a group such as a monastery primarily oriented to economic profit, the purpose of the monastery would be subverted. In terms of monastic ideals, the economic orientation would be immoral. Or, for a family to function strictly as a business would mean that the husband and wife would have to prostitute themselves to each other, while the children would have to pay for (or owe for) their room, board, and education. Communal organizations are based on a principle which in the ultimate sense can (and does) attain unilateral sacrifice, and this is the principle of love.

## LOVE AND COMMITMENT

The analysis now returns to the first hypothesis: If a group gives primacy to specific goals, it excludes the family. The problem with this hypothesis should now be clearer: the hypothesis is formulated too specifically. As stated, the hypothesis may be quite relevant for some kinds of groups in some situations, but it is not substantiated when applied to a large number of different groups. The hypothesis may now be reformulated in light of the preceding discussion to read: Formal organizations tend to exclude love relationships. The ideal-typical analysis has suggested that formal organizations are indifferent to love relationships—until, that is, the love relationships interfere with the primacy of the specific goal. The hypothesis cannot be scientifically verified as it is given, since love is not a scientific concept. A testable hypothesis may be deduced from it: Groups established on the basis of love should have members that are more committed than groups not so established. Communal organizations should have members that are more committed than members of formal organizations.

Commitment can be conceived as having at least two subtypes: involvement and cohesion. The data show that the communal organizations in this study are both more involved and more cohesive than the formal organizations.[10] Thus, the commitment in communal organizations is what one would expect if, as the ideal-typical analysis indicates, these organizations are based on love relationships. A qualification may be in order: There is no intention of claiming that all communal organizations are more committed than all formal organizations. The data show an overlap. The main point is that the findings concerning commitment are in agreement with the hypothesis concerning organization and love.

## FREEDOM, LOVE, AND COMMUNITY

Ladislaus Boros has said that the proper name of freedom "in its deepest sense is, after all, love."[11] In order for one to act in the best interest of the beloved, one must be *free* to do so. The more freedom (and the less coercion), the greater the extent to which love can be exercised. Since we have seen evidence to suggest that communal organization is the realization of freedom, then it follows that freedom, love, and community form a basic unity. We cannot conclude that this unity necessarily exists in all cases. There are communal organizations without love, but the unity is inherent in these concepts such that each attains its fullest realization only in union with the other two.

Freedom has its greatest realization in communal organizations, and it is greater in communal organizations than in informal groups. This is so because the fullest attainment of freedom is possible only with commitment, that is, with discipline. The reasoning behind such a statement is as follows: Ego freedom lives on the basis of having unhindered choices. Once a choice is made, other choices are ruled out. Making a choice—that is, realizing freedom—means imposing a discipline in the sense of ruling out other choices. Making a choice requires commitment. It follows that one will be able to make deeper commitments and thus realize more freedom to the extent that one is disciplined, and discipline requires rules. Thus, groups with more rules will be potentially capable of more freedom than those with fewer rules; so communal organizations will be potentially freer than informal groups.

The relation between freedom and love has been analyzed in the ideal types of the family and the monastery. The marital pair making the greatest commitment to each other (thus having the most love) also has the greatest freedom. The monk goes even further. In giving his life to his God, in forsaking not only all others but all things insofar as he is able, he also attains, theoretically, the greatest freedom. He is, to the extent that he is successful, free not only of the constraints of all others, but also of all else, all things. If he reaches the stage of complete freedom—the Buddhist *satori* or the Christian divine union—nothing binds him. Yet, paradoxically, everything binds him, because in his attainment of love he submits to all others and all else in love. It is a detachment that brings involvement, but the detachment is possible only in freedom.

The relation between love and community has been little more than implicit and remains to be sketched now, if only briefly. First we should note that the relation has been recognized by community theorists ever since Toennies, particularly in the form of community sentiment. The contribution to be offered here is in emphasizing the potential, not the necessity,of the connection. Communal organization does not necessarily mean community sentiment.[12] But in the same sense as freedom is related to community, so is love. For example, in the joining of two or more people to one another purely because they love one another and for no specific (i.e., measurable) reason, we find an essence of community. The peak experience is not necessarily there. The people so bound (but free) may not emote or celebrate continually. In fact, we would not expect them to. But the basis of the celebration, of the peak experience, is there, not only in the bonds that have grown through daily living, but also in the freedom with which those bonds have been forged, and continue to be.

Freedom, love, and community do not necessarily come together. The correlations in my data between freedom and community are not perfect. So it is in human experience: husbands murder wives, wives divorce husbands, communities engage in internecine feuds (reputedly the bloodiest kind), and communities of various sorts—families, villages, cities, nations—place stifling constraints on their members. This is to be expected, in the sense of a necessary evil: For freedom to be real, there must be non-freedom.[13]

## CONCLUSIONS

The ideal types as a whole point out several important variables of communal organizations which are difficult or impossible to phrase in a scientific manner. Communal organizations are groups which can maximize freedom and to which love is essential. It is possible for a communal organization to do without either of these for a while, but eventually any such deficiency, whether in the name of efficiency or expediency, will mean the death of the system. Loss of love in the ideal type will obviously mean the death of the marital unit; loss of freedom will obviously mean the death of the monastery. Even should such groups continue in outward form, the death would be apparent. For example, consider the married couple who constitute a business partnership and who are seeking a divorce (but not a dissolution of the partnership); consider the monastery becoming a prison. Though both groups may continue, they are dead or dying in their original state. But in a more subtle way, loss of freedom means the death of the marriage, just as loss of love means the death of the monastery. Should either partner in a marriage force the other into any act, then love is to that extent gone, and so is the marriage. The monk who can love neither his God nor other people is no longer a monk.

The discussion of ideal types also shows the importance of detachment in any form of love, from erotic to agapeic. It shows the essential inhumanity of formal organizations. That these considerations are not scientific is admitted, but they began with a scientific basis,[14] and they proceed to encompass elements which I have tried to argue are indispensable to the survival of the system. Extending scientific discussions into areas of truth that are not scientific forces us to raise questions and search for answers that are crucial to the existence of humanity, not to mention science itself.

Theological truth has been largely neglected in this discussion, but at least one observation in this area can be offered. Monks have developed disciplined freedom as much or more than any other group considered here. Of the twelve groups with the highest scores on disciplined freedom, all but two had one hundred percent of their members believing in God.[15]

A continuum of freedom may be proposed, beginning with egoistic freedom, which is purely self-centered and concentrated on the physical world. Conditional freedom is still oriented toward the physical world but is centered on other things and people. Disciplined freedom, like egoistic freedom, is oriented toward the self, but for an entirely different reason. The theme of disciplined freedom is sacrifice and sharing. Taking a cue from the extremely high scores for disciplined freedom achieved by monks,[16] the proposition is advanced that true disciplined freedom is centered on spiritual truth, which for the monks studied here means Jesus Christ. The monk disciplines his self in order to attain the freedom Christ offers.

Disciplined freedom, then, is but a means to an end—unconditional freedom: for the monk, that type which is oriented outward from the self and toward Christ in an ideal-typical sense. This is the freedom of which theologians and mystics speak when they say that one who has the mind of Christ can do as she or he pleases—the common source for which is probably the popular rendering of St. Augustine: "Love and do what you will."[17]

The importance of love and freedom to communal organizations may be used to expand the ideas presented in terms of a general taxonomy of human groups. William J. Goode has proposed "four great social control systems in all societies"—force (or power), wealth, prestige, and love.[18] The hypothesis has now been raised that considerations of love and freedom are not entirely relevant to formal organizations. Nevertheless, it follows from the nature of the goals of formal organizations, that force, wealth, and prestige *are* quite pertinent mechanisms of social control for these kinds of groups. Two extreme systems of control may be postulated. At one extreme, systems are operated purely in terms of power, wealth, and prestige. At the other extreme, are systems operated purely in terms of love and freedom. Most groups have a mixture of both forms, but there are differing emphases. Formal organizations tend toward the use of power, prestige, and wealth. Communal organizations tend toward the use of freedom and love. I am not saying that communal organizations are all sweetness and light. Love and freedom are conditions that communal organizations *tend* to use, whereas formal organizations *tend* to use the other types.

One may argue, after Emile Durkheim, that a formal organization has its own moral code, as moral for its purposes as those of communal organizations. The formal organization seeks efficiency and justice, whereas the communal organization seeks love and mercy. There is no argument with this position. The argument is rather one of hegemony and dominance. We live in an age heavily controlled by formal organizations, and this means that efficiency and justice (which are impersonal) may often come before love and mercy. To the extent that such dominance prevails, humanity is in a precarious position.

Formal organizations, especially in the ideal-typical sense used here, are not conducive to the welfare of human beings, particularly if they are not mitigated by communal organizations. There is no way to prove this statement scientifically, because the word "welfare"—especially if based on love—is not a scientific term. Nevertheless, the depersonalization of formal organizations should now be evident. The only saving grace is that formal organizations are operated by humans, but as numerous scholars since Durkheim have indicated, the human group has an existence *sui generis*. Formal organizations, for all their seductive utility, can have the power to cause us to act impersonally toward one another, and impersonal behavior is not in the best interest of humanity.[19]

# 8. The Power of Prayer: Observations and Possibilities

*William H. Swatos, Jr.*

For a variety of reasons the sociology of religion has rarely dealt with the phenomenon of prayer. Occasionally authors have commented on this and offered speculative explanations.[1] What they suggest is that the positivistic origins of sociology have created a bias against granting any empirical credence to prayer at all. If as sociologists—in our "sociologist role" as it is often termed—we must be somewhere between atheists and agnostics,[2] then prayer is an "unreasonable" act unworthy of our professional attention. Perhaps psychologists can study it as a mental state, but sociologists can learn little here. Prayer—beyond either sex or suicide, which were quickly subsumed under the canons of scientific rationality—becomes the final, ultimately irrational act. Of course, this is a caricature—but not so much as to be a slander. How people have behaved in and about worship has been studied in myriad ways, but what they said was largely ignored; it could have been jibberish. Indeed, far more attention has been given to the utterances of glossolaliacs than to those who speak plainly.

Yet even cursory reflection yields data which demonstrate that prayer is a thoroughly social activity. Not only is there a great deal of public prayer, but even that aspect of prayer designated as "private" is conditioned by and responsive to the interaction people have in day-to-day life with their fellows. Human face-to-face interaction is the model, in fact, for virtually all prayer: a talking or listening to someone. Whereas reality is a social construction and sociologists are to take the taken-for-granted knowledge of their subjects as *real* knowledge, it is irrelevant to discuss the existence of the posited receiver/transmitter at the "other end" of human prayer. *People* pray, and that is all a sociologist needs to know in order to begin work.[3]

Here, too, a preliminary caveat needs to be entered: If we are to develop a sociology of prayer with the greatest theoretical potential, then prayer must not be definitionally limited to its professionalized sense—that practiced by hermits, cloistered monastics, or other trained religious (though this should not be ignored either)—but in its pretheoretical *common*sense, as an activity open to everyone. Jacques Ellul's *Prayer and Modern Man* begins from a partially sociological starting point, but is actually a religious critique of prayer in its common sense, and thus not really congenial to what I propose.[4] Hundreds of millions of people in the Western world pray sometime(s) in their lives—many often, with various degrees of seriousness. What this involves for them and for others is the subject of our inquiry.

## PRAYER AND POWER

Practically all prayer in the Western tradition is directed toward a being who is considered to be rational and responsible. In that sense, this receiver/transmitter is termed *personal*, and interaction with this being is therefore possible. For many, of course, there is far more to the character of the receiver/transmitter than this, but for our purposes this minimum suffices. To some, the receiver/transmitter is "out there"; to others, "in here." That, too, matters little at this time. My argument is that from a sociological point of view, one of the most important characteristics of the receiver/transmitter is *power*, and that practically all prayer is an intentional encounter with power. Power to change things, power to keep things as they are, power to make things bearable, power to love, power to forgive, power adored.[5] If at least one definition of sociology is that it is the study of power relationships between people or among groups of people, then a sociology that has excluded this dimension of power for a wide segment of human society is to that extent an inadequate sociology.[6] In these pages I hope to provide some development and illustration of this thesis drawn from experiences as both participant-observer and observing-participant in prayer life.

One of the most characteristic exercises of Christian ascetics is meditation on the Lord's Prayer—the prayer that the New Testament claims Jesus explicitly taught his disciples to offer. It can also provide a base for this investigation. Through a line-by-line analysis, we can see that practically every phrase has power implications. "Our Father who art in heaven," sets the stage for:

(1) Hallowed be thy name: God's name is awesome.
(2) Thy Kingdom come: God is ruler—power of judgment.
(3) Thy will be done: Intentional power (norms).
(4) Give us . . . daily bread: Power over matter.
(5) Forgive . . . as we forgive: Power to facilitate order.
(6) Lead us not into temptation: Power to prevent wrong.
(7) Deliver us from evil: Power to prevent ultimate loss.

The concluding doxology which is usually added is nothing more than an unremitting celebration of power.

Power-related themes also emerge in the even less sectarian "Serenity Prayer," in which God is asked to grant the supplicant courage to change the changeable, serenity to accept the unchangeable, and wisdom to discern between the two. Here the receiver/transmitter grants to the human supplicant personal ("inner") strength, the ability to act on convictions, and knowledge of life's affairs. Coping with life becomes a matter of establishing a connection to a higher source of power. Saying the Serenity Prayer may bring "peace of mind," but it is also an admission that the individual alone is powerless to control either the events of history or his or her own destiny. The therapeutic use of this prayer in Alcoholics Anonymous is manifest: The individual at one and the same time admits his or her own powerlessness to deal with the problem and the existence of a "higher Power" upon which life depends.

From these two examples, multiple power dimensions (or foci) to prayer may be proposed in taxonomic fashion:

(1) Power-in-itself. This is the prayer of adoration, in which some power aspect of the receiver/transmitter is contemplated for its own sake. Prayer motivated by *love* is included here. A more "real world" analogy would be that of observing a waterfall or ocean breakers merely for the image or "feeling" of power they convey. No thought would be given, for example, to their usefulness in

providing electrical energy in a practical way. Prayer of adoration is frequently considered by ascetic theologians the highest form of prayer, and sociologically we would acknowledge that it utterly transcends the means-end schema.

(2) Power *ex machina*. This prayer asks that the receiver/transmitter act from outside the empirical world, either to change things or keep them as they are when they might otherwise be changed. Such prayers would include both benediction and intercession. Prayers for rain, prayers to heal, blessings of public buildings, prayers to destroy enemies, prayers to "bring the boys home" would all be included here.

(3) Power within. More in the character of the Serenity Prayer, the receiver/transmitter is asked to give to the supplicant or some other individual or group a heightening of human powers they already possess. Outside intervention is not the goal. Rather, human potential must be fully actualized—and apparently some superhuman "push" is necessary to complete or impede this process. A "higher power" is a precondition to full human power. For some, indeed, this power dependency or "creatureliness" becomes definitional for human being or true humanity.

(4) Posthumous power. In this category I put not prayers "to" the departed (i.e., the intercession of saints)—most of which are of the *ex machina* category—but those offered to a receiver/transmitter which are intended to improve the state of the departed in the netherworld. These are somewhat similar to *ex machina* prayers. Since the departed "souls" are no longer in the empirical universe, however, the display of power requested is of a different order. A person who could not conceive of a receiver/transmitter changing the course of events in empirical history might still view the receiver/transmitter as powerful in this way *and vice versa*. Posthumous power is a separate category, then, because it does not anticipate that the receiver/ transmitter will display power in an empirically falsifiable way. A seance would *not* be included here either, since a primary criterion for its success would be that the departed is "brought back" into the empirical world.[7]

(5) Power acknowledged. Thanksgivings and some blessings fall into this category. Although it may appear that this is but a form of power-in-itself, two qualities seem to differentiate it. First, thanksgivings are specific. The receiver/transmitter is acknowledged

for doing or preventing something. Often, admittedly, thanksgivings begin with a power-in-itself thanking God for being God; following that, however, there is also a particular reason which calls forth—and so legitimates—the giving of thanks at that specific time. Second, thanksgivings carry within them intercessions. An offering of thanks always asks that the status quo for which thanks is being offered either be maintained or improved. How this is to be done will depend upon whether the original intercession (if there were one) was *ex machina* or within in character. Food blessings are probably the most frequently offered prayers of this category. In traditional Jewish "graces," for example, the prayers begin, "Blessed be God..." Humanity "returns thanks" to God by acknowledging his creative power, but humanity also asks that the sustenance be continued. The nonsectarian children's grace "God is great, God is good, and we thank Him for our food," is very similar, although the intercession here remains completely implicit. Also included here is the eucharistic dismissal, "Let us bless the Lord/Thanks be to God." Whether a blessing will be *ex machina* or a prayer of acknowledgment depends largely upon whether the theology of the supplicant deems the item to be blessed created by the receiver/transmitter or through some other means. *Ex machina* blessings arise in direct proportion to dualism.

This five-way distinction permits the listing of many empirical subcategories, only a few of which have been mentioned above. Most prayers, like the Lord's Prayer, include elements from more than one class. There is thus no sense in which these distinctions are mutually exclusive in practice. A typical prayer during serious illness, for example, is likely to admire God's power, bid healing from outside, ask for inner strength, give thanks for previous health, and (just in case) commend the soul of the afflicted to "growth in grace beyond the veil."[8]

Prayers also generally include "informational material." The supplicant tells the receiver/transmitter something of the circumstances surrounding the communication and/or reminds the receiver/transmitter of some characteristic(s) pertaining to its being. This latter strategy may be an attempt to introduce some parity into the power-dependence relationship of deity to supplicant (e.g., the Pharisee in the New Testament parable of the Pharisee and the publican) or merely a legitimation of the request by specifying the condition under which the prayer is made. Occasionally informational material may form the entirety of a prayer. Even here, though, there is the underlying assumption that the receiver has the power at least to understand and usually also to act in some way upon circumstances so reported. In public prayer, this also functions to acquaint others (the crowd or congregation) with particulars that justify the offering of prayer on the occasion.[9] These may be unique, as at the dedication of a university's art gallery, or general, as the institution narrative in any eucharistic canon.

An essential observation follows: Practically all prayer assumes that there is a receiver who "hears" the prayer and who is capable of making a response. In ascetical theology this is often referred to as "listening for God's answer" or "waiting upon God." Except for totally therapeutic forms of prayer within or for pure adoration, prayer is deemed a two-way street, at least some of the time (i.e., there are debates *re* whether God answers all prayers, etc.).

This aspect of prayer life is what leads me to refer to the one(s) to whom prayer is addressed as receiver/ *transmitter*(s). I strongly suspect as well that it is this aspect of prayer as social action that gives many sociologists—whether personally religious or not—difficulty studying prayer as sociologists. To some, it would appear, merely to posit the existence of a receiver/transmitter is already to some extent to affirm one, and thus exceeds the canons of scientific agnosticism or "methodological atheism."[10] I would argue to the contrary that this is nothing more than to treat the taken-for-granted knowledge of social actors as reality for the purposes of social research. To suggest that some human behaviors might be the result of prayer, furthermore, is in itself no less scientific an explanation than are biological and physical theories based upon constructs whose reality cannot be falsified or affirmed except by derivation. Ironically, again, anthropologists have been able to do this for so-called primitive cultures for decades with relative ease, rarely if ever falling "prey" to their subjects' religious convictions. Only in modernity does the "existence" of a receiver/transmitter seem to become a potential threat to social scientific analysis.

## PRAYER AND EMPIRICISM

From here we can move to the question of whether prayer "works." This, too, seems a matter beyond empiricism. Formulated in this way, perhaps it is. But it can be reformulated in ways that admit falsification. To do so is to ask questions of how prayer is supposed to work, how supplicants pray, how supplicants act when prayer "works" and when it doesn't, how prayer is used in social relationships. To a very limited extent there are investigations that have touched on these issues—mostly, however, with regard to charismatics.[11] The classic study on prophecy by Festinger and his associates might serve as a model here.[12] Bellah's initial essay on civil religion can likewise be seen as a study, in part, of how invocations of the deity in presidential addresses function in American politics, society, and culture.[13] But these are just the tip of a potentially huge research iceberg. Maximum explanatory value from our research will come only when prayer is studied for itself in comparative context—i.e., what differences in attitudes and action appear (1) when prayer is present or absent, (2) when different forms of prayer occur, (3) in the same or different sociocultural strata or settings? Several empirical observations may illustrate this point.

I have observed many small group interactions in which people revealed hidden aspects of their personalities (e.g., sensitivity groups). In these I have noted that prayer-based groups have in general a more positive emphasis in terms of future social interaction, whereas the secular group tends to be more negative. The prayer group tends to work toward a facilitation of supportive social action for all concerned, whereas the other groups emphasize individuation and assertiveness (e.g., "If people don't like me the way I am, they can go to hell."). This is true regardless of the physical locus, sponsorship, or leadership of the group. I would hypothesize that the more positive resolution occurs in the prayer-oriented group because the "revelation of self" occurs to others only indirectly. The primary recipient of the communication is the receiver/transmitter. The others in the group then support the supplicant, who is in turn not goaded into asserting personal identity in order to preserve threatened integrity. Rather, the supplicant becomes positively united to the others as a "support group," all of the members of which have stood or anticipate standing in this relationship to the receiver/transmitter. At the same time, if the group maintains a consciousness of the transcendent supremacy of the receiver/transmitter, it is discouraged from gnostic exclusiveness and potential antagonism toward the rest of society.

Several years ago one of my students and I engaged in the systematic observation of prayers offered at a Y.M.C.A.-sponsored "new games" sports program for children. The emphasis of "new games" is specifically upon playing and game-learning, rather than on competitiveness (i.e., winning and losing, team standings, "star" players). The program we studied was awarded regional recognition (the Southeast) as an outstanding example of this strategy. Before each match in the program, participants and parents were gathered into a circle by a staff member who would be refereeing the game. There were mutual greetings, the youngsters would be asked if one had a joke or special story to tell, and then the staff member would ask if someone would pray. If no parent-figure volunteered (children never did so), the staff member offered the prayer. Although the prayers sometimes only celebrated good weather and youthful energies, more often the prayer was a medium for reminding everyone of the nature of the program and of appropriate and inappropriate actions and attitudes. The technique of involving the participants' parents with the staff member, rather than a religious professional, introduced an implicit self-control mechanism that not only reinforced the "rules of the game," but also created a *consensus fidelium* about the rightness of what was happening. A similar function is served by the traditional prayer offered by a Roman Catholic priest as he puts on his rope girdle in vesting for Mass: "Gird me, 0 Lord, with the girdle of purity, and extinguish in me all concupiscence."

Prayers are obviously an important element in formal worship. In churches with fixed liturgies, we can easily analyze the various themes, expectations, and functions involved. What is important to recognize is that in so-called "free" churches, the same ordered style develops. One informant reared in a free tradition reported that teenagers in the church reduced the pastor's potential prayer options to a numbered series. They would then lay bets on the actual series and its order in a given worship service! One cannot observe free church worship for long without realizing that certain themes, expectations, and functions are considered appropriate and others inappropriate for offering in prayer at worship, and that these constellations *vary* with sociocultural indicators such as socioeconomic status, education, or race.

I have already mentioned the place of prayer in the context of civil religion, and this obviously is capable of great expansion both in the United States and crossculturally. One can ask, for example, what Franklin the deist was trying to accomplish when he proposed that sessions of Congress begin with prayer (as they have ever since his motion carried). Or, on a more contemporary note, one can ask what power the political prayer breakfast has in the affairs of state in the 1980s. This social behavior at the highest levels of earthly power deserves more than a shrug or a snigger.

Another aspect of prayer in the nation-state arena, however, may be suggested by reference to the fulminations of the Reverend Ian Paisley in Northern Ireland. In a prayer widely televised in late 1981, for example, Paisley not only called the wrath of God down upon the enemies of the Protestant partisans, but also called upon God to give their movement strength to destroy Catholicism—apparently in Northern Ireland first, then throughout the world.[14] One wonders, too, about the role of prayer in prohibition or the more recent successes of the Moral Majority in the United States. Are crusades in any era undertaken because they are preached or prayed (or both or neither)? What effect did the fact that 1960s activists were often stopped *from praying* have upon the outcome of their efforts? In short: How much social energy is engaged by calling upon the deity that would not be so engaged otherwise? One can cite Deutsch's empirical finding that national consciousness develops among a people whenever there is an assertion of birthrights for everybody "*first in the language of religion*, then in the language of politics, and finally in terms involving economics and all society," and wonder how much further this may be generalized.[15] To what extent, then, does committing a political concern to prayer extend the power of that concern to motivate people? And under what circumstances? *Who* must pray and *when* for this to happen?

Finally, though it may be more far-fetched as a research strategy, it seems potentially possible to investigate experimentally how prayer works: Many denominational and interdenominational groups hold summer conferences involving hundreds or thousands of people. Some of these same groups have research staffs in their employ or available to them. Often small groups play some role in these meetings. Careful advance planning could result in random assignment of participants to different groups in which prayers were present or absent, leader or participant based, individual or corporate, and so forth. By a sensitive awareness to session goals and group processes across a number of "trials," it might well be possible to specify the kinds of conditions under which prayer is or is not effective or the relationship of different kinds of prayer to different outcomes or anticipated outcomes. This may raise ethical questions for some, but it is difficult to see how this any more violates ethical norms than other religious research on human subjects—including research in parish or church-organizational contexts, which has been ongoing in one form or another for many decades.

## CONCLUSION

A favorite sermon illustration on the power of prayer tells the story—possibly apocryphal, possibly not—of the impoverished post-revolutionary Russian peasant whose family was starving. He gathered them around the table to pray, not knowing that outside stood some of Stalin's troops. Observing the prayer through the window, one soldier tossed a loaf of bread down the chimney. The family pounced on it, thanked God, and started to eat. The soldiers suddenly burst in and exclaimed, "What fools you are! You think God sent you that food from heaven, but instead Ivan here threw it down the chimney." "Oh?," said the father, "Fools? We're eating aren't we?"

It is a characteristic of such rhetorical illustrations that the story ends without telling anything of subsequent events—which might well have been gruesome. I introduce it here as a final example of what is involved in the question of whether prayer "works." This and all the preceding illustrative material are meant to suggest the kinds of strategies and hypotheses that can reasonably become part of the sociology of prayer. One could certainly think of others: "The family that prays together stays together" is an empirically falsifiable proposition. There are alternative approaches to healing.[16] Prayer has long been associated with the grief process.

In this essay, I have tried to stimulate investigation of prayer as a sociologically relevant variable that can be studied without abandoning such "virtues" as value neutrality or methodological atheism. Whereas prayer is a central religious attitude and action that has been and is engaged in by millions of people across time, place, and circumstance—indeed, it may be the most universal religious variable—to ignore or degrade it as a valid object for sociological investigation and theory is hopelessly and needlessly to obfuscate the empirical manifestation of religion in society. Such an approach is an intellectualization and professionalization of the religious variable that fails to meet the minimal sociological criterion that a situation *is* what it is defined to be by its participant actors, and that religious situations are in this respect no different from any other.[17]

# 9. The Invisible Religion of Catholic Charismatics

## Pierre Hegy

The relationship between scientific knowledge and popular wisdom is a central issue for the interpretive, "hermeneutic" sciences. It was Plato who first raised the question of the relationship between *epistémé* (specialized knowledge) and popular culture. There are at least three ways we know things, he asserts: as they exist in "nature," as they are known by artesans and producers, and as they are reproduced in the arts.[1] Similarly, there are at least three images or "names" for things given by different social groups, which might impose their image of reality: the law makers, the creator-producers, and the consumers.[2] Which social construction of reality should prevail today, we may ask: that of sociologists and social scientists, or that of popular knowledge and popular wisdom?

There are at least three ways, following Plato still, or modes to relate scientific knowledge to popular culture. There is, first, the *educational mode* according to which science is "insight" or inner enlightenment; education is the process of inner enlightenment. This is Plato's position. According to the *Myth of the Cave* every human being must grapple with the darkness of human knowledge, the scholar (e.g., the mathematician in *Meno* or the sociologist), as well as the uneducated (the slave in *Meno* or the sociologist's subjects). It is only through the inner enlightenment of philosophy (wisdom) that one will come closer to the "light" of truth. In this perspective, the sociological construction of society must remain in constant dialogue with other symbolic constructions. There is also the *instructional mode* according to which science is truth, and popular knowledge is seen as ignorance; learning here is "brain feeding" on information. This conception of knowing has prevailed since the advent of "modern" science in the eighteenth century and the subsequent development of mass instruction. How can sociologists relate to their subjects in this perspective? A common answer is found in the distinction between empathy and sympathy: the sociologists must show *empathy* toward different symbolic constructions, but must remain aloof and distant from these worldviews.[3] Such a position is quite untenable. "In the last analysis," wrote Robbins and Anthony over a decade ago, "the empathy/sympathy distinction is not completely tenable because one cannot fully comprehend what one has not personally experienced."[4] Methodological empathy is inspired by the intellectual arrogance of the instructional mode according to which science is truth and nonscience is ignorance. Finally, there is also the *debunking mode*, when non-science is seen, not just as ignorance, but as prejudice or false knowledge. Here science takes on a pseudo-religious mission of "saving" the world from its illusion (e.g., Lundberg). The debunking mode is quite common in sociology. When a feeling of superiority animates the researcher, he or she can show little "empathy" for other people's "prejudice."

In this essay, I will write within the framework of the educational mode, taking for granted that the hermeneutic sciences must remain in constant dialogue with popular wisdom. But how will such a dialogue be possible? Who will speak in the name of "popular culture"? The answer to this question, in a democratic society, can be found in the theory of representativity. It is a basic principle of democratic representation that a representative be allowed to speak for those he or she represents. A political representative must know the needs and wishes of the constituency, in order to represent their interests truly. An envoy expresses the wishes of his master, not his own. Similarly a lawyer speaks for her client and may plead the client "not guilty" even when she knows the evidence is against the client. Although an attorney speaks for her client, she never identifies herself with her client: no lawyer will go to jail to take the place of a convicted customer. The same principle of representativity is applied in the social sciences in statistical form. When taking a random sample, we believe that the answers of the respondents "represent" the position of the whole population. The social scientist can then speak in the name of the whole population, because of a trust in the sample as "representative."

In this paper I will speak "in the name" of those studied. Because I did not use a random sample but followed the anthropological method of participant observation, there can be no "scientific" claim of representativity. The groups I will try to "represent" are Charismatic prayer groups in Long Island. I will give more information on these groups in the course of discussion.

In this essay I want to answer some of the following questions: What are the shortcomings of sociology of religion in the opinion of those with whom I interacted? Which aspect of the religious experience has been ignored or undervalued by the sociologists? Which sociological concepts make little sense to these respondents?

## THE INVISIBLE RELIGION

The major criticism leveled against sociology by lay people is that we seldom go beyond the surface; we discover only what is obvious. More specifically, sociologists of religion do not go beyond what is "visible," ignoring the invisible nature of religion. It is precisely this invisible nature of religion that Charismatics claim to have rediscovered. What is a religious act? Not necessarily what might be measured in 5-D scales.[5] Visible religion, Charismatics claim, may be invalidated by ritualism, traditionalism, shallowness, hypocrisy.

What is a religious group or congregation? It does not necessarily consist of those present at a religious meeting, because the "true church" is invisible. At any given prayer meeting, some important members may be absent. At most prayer meetings, references are made to outside events: retreats, readings, meetings at other churches, even secular events. At any meeting, there are prayers for the absent, the sick, and the poor. Religious groups include not only the living but also the dead, not only the present but also the past and the future, which constantly interface with our present, not only the ordinary members but also the famous writers and saints, who constitute the reference group of the assembly. The visible boundaries of the established churches have become meaningless: one finds Catholic pentecostals at Holiness meetings and vice versa; even the boundaries between Judaism and Christianity have become blurred. It is the invisible nature of these boundaries in the groups I have studied which constitutes their major characteristic. I have been a sociological "participant" in a Catholic prayer group of about 300 to 500 members for about two years, and also in various non-Catholic prayer groups in Long Island. It is startling to find members of one group participate in events organized by another group as if the religious boundaries had become meaningless. The constant "switching" which takes place is not from one denomination or church to another, but from the visible church to an "invisible" one. The "church," it seems, has become "invisible," at least for the Charismatics.

## THE INVISIBLE CHURCH

What is a "church" or religious community? What do churches say about themselves? Since the average believer is not likely to be able to answer this question for the whole, we have to turn to the theologians and intellectuals who are present as a reference group through their writings on display on the "book table." Karl Rahner was among the first within Catholicism to define Christianity as an invisible community of believers scattered all over the world, in a state of "diaspora," like the Jews after the destruction of Jerusalem. The one, visible, and hierarchical church of the Middle Ages has been destroyed; instead there are pluralistic, invisible, and egalitarian communities.[6] More revolutionary still is Câmara's notion of an "ecumenical humanism," which begins with the Abrahamic community of Jews, Muslims, and Christians but reaches out to all who respond in faith to God's inner calling of service to humanity— even if, as nontheists, they do not acknowledge an external source.[7] Only slightly less radically, Vatican II redefined the "church" as "the people of God," including all people of good will, whatever religion or creed they profess (or do not profess). According to this official document, the true church only "subsists" in the Catholic church, being understood that it also "subsists" in many other churches.[8] The conception of an "invisible church" has been systematized by Avery Dulles in his popular *Models of the Church*. This work is inspired by the sociological method of "ideal types." The author distinguishes five "models." Only the first, the institutional church, refers to a visible organization. Such a model, however, is obsolete. It belongs to "the age of the monolithic Church, which aspired to a single universal language (Latin), a single theological system (Neo-Scholasticism), a single system of worship (the Roman rite), and a single system of government (the Code of Canon Law)."[9] All other models of the church refer to an "invisible" entity: the church as Mystical Communion, Sacrament, Herald, and Servant.

Evidence from participant observation makes it obvious that today most believers in most religious organizations adhere to a conception of the church as invisible and universal. But only one or two generations ago, membership in the institutional churches was as strict as in private clubs during prohibition. Excommunication and refusal of the sacraments were real threats—e.g., in the Roman Catholic church in case of divorce. Today, by contrast, it is customary to welcome warmly occasional visitors and non-members. It is also customary in many prayer groups to publicize religious events taking place in other prayer groups of whatever denomination. Behind this change lies not only a greater tolerance, and maybe a greater indifference, but also a different ecclesiology: Religious groups, probably for the first time in the West, claim that all people of good will (believers and non-believers —even sociologists) can belong to the "invisible church." Yet, sociological theorizing has not followed.

If I were to speak for those I have studied, I would say that our intricacies about the church-sect typology, for example, are totally unpalatable to today's Charismatics. This typology seems a legacy of the time of Weber and Troeltsch, without relevance to our changed world. No more relevant is the distinction between *Gemeinschaft* and *Gesellschaft*. Actually there has been little or no theorizing about the notion of "religious community." A church is not essentially a bureaucracy, although it may exhibit many bureaucratic features. It is not essentially a legal institution, like a firm or corporation, although it may use its legal status to financial advantage. It is not just a voluntary association, since non-members may belong to the "invisible church." It may be defined as a "covenant"—as conceived by the seventeenth and eighteenth century Covenant theology of New England; yet such a theology is generally unknown in sociological circles.[10]

## THE INVISIBLE SACRED AND THE INVISIBLE PROFANE

Our sociological theorizing is still informed by the traditional dichotomy between the sacred and the secular, inherited from Kant and Schleiermacher. This dichotomy was popularized in theological circles by Rudolf Otto, in anthropology and sociology by Mauss and Durkheim, and more recently in comparative religion by Mircea Eliade.[11] According to this view, the sacred is supposedly experienced as something totally different from the secular. According to Otto, the divine is experienced as something "wholly different" (*ganz andere*), as a frightening mystery (*mysterium tremendum*) which inspires "stupor."[12] The same dichotomy is found in the opposition between the sacred space, where the divine rests, and secular space—or between sacred and secular times. Mauss and Durkheim have illustrated this dichotomy among the Eskimos and the Australian primitives.

This dichotomy is totally contradicted by everyday life evinced through participant observation research. A prayer group may meet, for instance, in a basement, or a living room, as well as in a small chapel. When the group splits—for instance to pray for healing in small groups—some may pray in the boiler room, others in the staircase, seldom in the church itself, as if a boiler room were more congenial to small group prayer than an enormous and empty church building.

From my participant observation I sense that a tremendous shift has been taking place in recent years: the *focus* of the sacred has shifted from the "sacred place" and sacred objects to the inner self. The sacred is experienced not as a frightening outside mystery, but as a friendly inner mystery, as a silent voice that can be heard in one's inner recess, as something more personal than one's most inner self. An illustration of this shift is found in the United States Catholic bishops' pastoral letter *The Challenge of Peace*: Nuclear war must be avoided because of the "sacredness of human life." We are responsible to "protect and preserve the sanctity of life," because "life is sacred."[13] Thus, "the central idea in the letter is the sacredness of human life," because human life is more sacred than gothic cathedrals, Hindu shrines, or Vatican museums.

For the Charismatics, to reject the sacred-secular dichotomy is to claim that nothing is actually secular. If the locus of the sacred is the inner self, then any human activity, any human creation, any collective or individual endeavor can be the occasion for a religious experience. This conception of the divine as an inner voice is most common in the Biblical tradition (e.g., Jeremiah being "inspired" while watching a potter at work), precisely because in Biblical times there was no dichotomy between the secular and the religious. There is no such dichotomy either, I believe, in Judaism and Buddhism.

## THE INVISIBLE SECULARIZATION

To the extent that religion is defined as an invisible experience, i.e., as "ultimate concern," the grand theory of Western secularization becomes questionable. No doubt, religious practices have decreased substantially; yet such decreases may prove only the decline of traditionalism, conventionality, and ritualism. The influence of religion has also decreased in many secular realms (education, politics, entertainment, and the like), but such a decline would be seen as beneficial by Charismatics, since the excessive concern with ultimate ends in the past has often inhibited the development of natural and technical means.[14] If secularization means the de-clericalization of the world, it is indeed progress. Yet in the variety of the many meanings of the term,[15] there is one dimension that has escaped most sociologists. It was Weber's major thesis that the Western world has increasingly become rationalized and disenchanted. He did not see such a development as "progress" but as tragedy—the tragedy of our "iron cage" of trivialized charisma.[16] The tragedy of Western rationalization and disenchantment, trivialization, has further been developed by Horkheimer and Marcuse.[17] Weber has clearly defined rationality (*Zweckrationalität*) as concerned only with "means," irrespective of any "ends." The excessive concern with "means" irrespective of "ends" found in modern science and our technological culture has produced a trivialized (secularized) world in which the production of nuclear arms, toxic gases, or deadly bombs is rationally planned like any other consumer good—from production to marketing. In that perspective, secularization as trivialization is a modern tragedy, because it has numbed our concern with ultimate ends, not only in religion, but also in poetry, the arts, philosophy, and all other forms of culture.

122 *Pierre Hegy*

## RELIGION AS INVISIBLE FAITH

To the extent that religion is essentially (but not only) an invisible experience, it has received little attention in sociological quarters in recent years. Religion has been conceived as "ultimate concern," but it was by a theologian of the previous generation, Paul Tillich. The religious has been again defined by Bellah as "a set of symbolic acts which relate man to the ultimate conditions of his existence."[18] In spite of the great influence of this general definition, however, it has not produced any significant theoretical development. Luckmann's conception of the "invisible religion," though obviously provocative, is equally vague.[19]

It is outside sociological circles that we find today the greatest development. Using the sociological technique of surveys and life-stories, James Fowler has developed "universal" stages of "faith development." At each stage we find not only Christians and Jews, but unbelievers as well. Faith development does not apply only to "children and women," or traditionalists and fundamentalists, but to all people of good or bad faith, whether they are "religious" or not.[20] Although Fowler's research takes place outside the sociology of religion, it is part of today's dynamic interest in developmental psychology and life cycles. That the invisible experience of religion is a dynamic process of faith development, as already pointed out by Tillich,[21] probably strikes at the core of the Charismatic experience. Many Catholic pentecostals see ritualism and traditionalism as stagnant and sterile phases of their past life, and as constant threats to their present life. That "faith" must constantly develop is one of their most basic beliefs. For them, "conversion" is seen as a continuous process, rather than a once-for-all accomplishment. With a greater awareness of the psychic forces that interfere in their own "conversion," they have come to recognize certain factors that impede such progress, e.g., ritualism, dogmatism, fear, inauthenticity, and so forth. To the extent that faith development is a universal phenomenon that can find its expression in religious as well as non-religious symbolism, the road seems open for a dialogue between various symbolic constructions of reality.

## CONCLUSION

I began this essay by pointing out that the relationship between popular wisdom and scientific knowledge is a vital issue in the hermeneutic sciences, to the extent that these sciences claim to reach "human significance," rather than mere statistical significance. Human significance and commonsense are supposedly equally distributed among all people, hence no special group—e.g., sociologists—can claim to reach greater insights. There are at least three modes for the cultural sciences to relate to popular knowledge, two of which are inspired by a claim of superiority on the part of scientists. In the educational mode, however, there is no such claim, although each group may claim to be superior in its own distinctive ways according to its own distinctive methods. The educational mode is one of dialogue between different symbolic constructions, each having its distinctive value. It is only when the validity of different symbolic constructions is recognized that one can learn from another.

The faith development theory, however, brings a new dimension into this dialogue. To the extent that "faith" is a universal—and not just a religious—phenomenon, it implicates all of us—as either Christians, or Jews, or unbelievers, sociologists, socialists, pacifists, or whatever. Traditionalism, dogmatism, or shallowness are obstacles in "faith development" as much in sociology as in religion, in interpersonal relations as in relating to oneself. As it stands today, faith development constitutes a vast program for both empirical research and theoretical formulation. Only further research can fulfill these hopes.

# 10. Militant Religion

## Eugen Schoenfeld

An oft-repeated sociological dictum is that religion is a conservative institution. It is taken almost as an axiom that religion supports the status quo, supports and legitimates the ruling elite, and demands and rewards submissiveness from the lower socioeconomic strata. Empirical findings, however, do not support such a unidirectional relationship. Wuthnow, for example, reviewing the literature on religion and politics, concludes that the evidence is indeed unclear, and the relationship between conservatism and politics is an elusive one. He found that while there were researches which reported a conservative relationship, there were others which found no such relationship, and still others which showed that religion tends to oppose conservatism and to deny support to the ruling power.[1] Indeed, as Lewy has observed, religion is Janus-faced.[2] Often religion (i.e., the clergy representing their religion's point of view), instead of being conservative, supports and advocates liberating theologies. On the other hand, it frequently rejects attempts to eliminate traditionalism and displays of opposition to the ruling elite. The question is: What makes some religions more militant, while others are docile and submissive to power?

## CONCEPTUALIZING THE PROBLEM

I would argue that the reason for the inconsistencies in the varied research reports is due to inadequate conceptualization. The two most frequently used approaches in such studies are the unidimensional approach, which includes both the Marxian and functionalist theories, and the multidimensional approach, which surveys dimensions of religiosity. Each of these approaches, in its own way, fails to differentiate the *Weltanschauungen* associated with a particular belief. Consequently, all of them are unable to understand or explain how different religious worldviews and associated values affect a particular religion's association with the political world.

Both functionalism and Marxism share a common perspective on religion and politics: that religion provides moral and ideological support for the status quo. Functionalists see this as necessary for continued social existence and thus as good ("value neutrality" notwithstanding); Marxists see it as bad. More important, both of these orientations advocate the ideas that: (1) religion is an undifferentiated entity, and (2) religion has a single consequence, evident in its relationship with power maintenance (Marxists) or social stability (functionalists). To the Marxist, religion—regardless of its theology, history, or size—is part of the Ideological Support Apparatus and as such reenforces the state,[3] which itself is the political arm of ruling class interest. Merton's elaboration of possible dysfunctionalities aside,[4] a functional perspective is likely to direct our attention to religion away from conflict but likewise (though more positively) to social reenforcement functions. Thus both perspectives enhance an indiscriminate view of religion "in general" and a theoretical frame which leads people to expect religion to support conservative politics.

In contrast to the unidimensional approach, the multidimensional method advocates a view in which religiosity is conceptualized as sets of different phenomena. The difficulty with this approach is that it is reductionistic on the one hand but still indiscriminate in its generality. A given dimension, for example, is treated as existing with hardly any reference to who or what is believed or worshipped, when, in what context, and so forth. Religion is not seen as something whole, but as a collection of only-possibly-related parts of general applicability. While this approach may come closer to the nature of religion as lived experience, it obscures the property of emergence; that is, it does not sensitize us to religion as an institution that cannot be fully understood if it is seen only in its separate constituent elements.[5]

The impact a particular religion has on an adherent's political view cannot be explained or understood as the consequence of a single dimension of religion. To understand such a relationship we need to approach religion from a *modified wholistic view*—not as an undifferentiated entity, nor as reduced and fragmented by surveys of "dimensions." The best model for insight into the relationship between religion and politics is the ideal type: a construct in which are incorporated various features that characterize and differentiate those religions that have a greater tendency toward militancy from those that stress subserviency.

## MILITANCY

Most historical and sociopolitical studies of militant religion have focused on situational factors that enhance religious opposition to the ruling elite. But not all religions facing the same political conditions will respond with militancy. Situation and leadership are also necessary for religious revolution; yet these two conditions are not in themselves sufficient. What differentiates those religions that are militant from accommodative and submissive religions are particular theological *Weltanschauungen* that arise out of and respond to the class conditions of their adherents.

The classic example of religious militancy is Old Testament prophecy. In the name of YHWH prophets opposed the ruling elite and questioned their power legitimacy. Thus, one aspect of militancy is a political dimension wherein religious leaders challenge the basis of the political leadership's legitimacy.[6] Another dimension that is central to militant religion is a commitment to change. If submissive religions are committed to the status quo, then militant ones are obviously seeking change from it. In this respect, however, militant religions differ. There are those that seek changes to conditions that have as yet not been—i.e., future oriented. By contrast, there are militant religions that are seeking to return to the paradise that has been lost. Finally, militant religions also differ with respect to inclusivity and exclusivity of membership. Religions that emphasize uniqueness and separation are to be differentiated from those where human commonality is emphasized.

A religion shall be termed inclusive to the extent that it emphasizes human and religious commonality—i.e., ecumenism in the broadest sense. Liberal religions, militant or not, are more likely to stress the idea of commonness. Militant religions, however, will emphasize this ideal in practice to a greater extent. On the other hand, exclusive militants—Christian, Jewish, or Moslem—emphasize the singular truthfulness of their religious view, the unique and distinct relationship members of their religion have with the deity, and the "jealousy" of God. These views justify them in seeing themselves as righteous and thereby in being punitive to those of other persuasions.

## RELIGION AND THE STATE

If there is one particular view that differentiates militant from submissive religions it is the legitimacy of the separation of church and state. The idea of rendering unto Caesar and God each's separate dues is the ideological infrastructure of the submissive religions. The legitimacy of secular power and its independence from religion—Pauline doctrine (Romans 13)—forms the basis for the separation of church and state. These two arenas have clear and distinct functions—one to be concerned with personal salvation in the world to come, the other with temporal concerns of the here and now. The common element of all militant religions is the rejection of this view. To the militant religions, religion consists not only of personal faith but also of associated acts. Both types of militant religions hold a view that social and political life must be subservient to an ethics that reflects the will of a higher authority.

The Old Testament prophets who epitomize religious militancy based their right to be critical of the ruling power on their relationship with the supernatural and on the demands of the supernatural, which must be given greater credence than the demands of political rulers.[7] That is, the foundation of religious militancy is incorporated in the idea that all people are first subject to the will of God. In addition to the idea of the will of God, the Western world has also been influenced by the concept of Natural Law. Although rooted in Catholic theology, the idea of Natural Law was given a different meaning by the eighteenth-century Philosophes.[8] Nature and the laws of nature have, in some instances, become a substitute for the laws of God. Like the law of God, the law of nature has been accepted as the true and right path on which society needs to be built. In essence, both the law of God and natural law include the idea that above the law that is found in statutes and a society's legal system there is a higher law, which has been given by God or which is part of a grander scheme of things called nature. The violation of such laws brings various forms of punishment. The violation of God's plan is associated with loss of His favor and subsequent punishments, as depicted in Deuteronomy. The violation of natural law similarly ends in disaster, for no people can subvert that which is essentially legitimate by right of nature.[9] A good example of these perspectives is Jerry Falwell's *Listen, America!*, where he repudiates the idea of separating Caesar's dues from the rest of life and preaches an active political commitment.

The subjugation of politics and civil authority to religion was also advocated by Calvin, who argues that "civil government has its appointed end...to prevent the true religion which is contained in God's law from being openly and with public sacrilege violated and defiled with impunity."[10] God and his law are the foundation of our civil, moral, and religious life. They are all interconnected, but God's will takes precedence. Thus Calvin held it to be blasphemy for Henry VIII to declare himself Supreme Head of the Church of England. By submitting oneself to the will of God, Caesar's will becomes secondary, and Caesar's behavior thus must be scrutinized, since the welfare of all depends more on the action of a nation's Caesar than any other single individual.

The idea of submission to a higher authority is also part of the liberal and inclusive-oriented religion. The difference is that inclusive religions perceive that the law that should guide people's lives is a universal law or morality. This view is a part of the foundation of nondenominational civil religion. Civil law and civil authority are not independent from higher authority, which is defined as the natural law that reflects the will of a universal and nondenominational diety. Criticism of civil authority thus is not based on an orthodox view of the law of God with its consequent commitment to a particularistic theocracy, but on a universal humanistic moral code.

## CLASS AND MILITANCY

My criticism of the Marxian perspective is based primarily on the over-emphasis of the dominant ideology thesis as articulated in *The German Ideology*.[11] This approach in Marxism has recently been criticized because of its incorporation of various historical inaccuracies.[12] In addition, however, there is a problem directly associated with this view's own political emphasis: Marxist sociologists have used this "theory" selectively to advocate the legitimacy of their own political agenda. Marx's theory, which is more germane to sociological analysis of religion, is that expressed in the preface to the *Critique of Hegel's Philosophy of Right* and the *Eighteenth Brumaire*:[13] Ideology and all aspects of the social superstructure are associated with and reflect people's position in the mode of production and different modes of property. To understand the nature of religious militancy and the distinction between inclusive and exclusive militancy, we need to relate it to the members' constituent class.

## Inclusive Militancy and Ascending Class

Militant religions espousing an inclusive orientation reflect the ideology of an ascending class. Whereas submissive religions with their other-worldly orientation and its emphasis on transvaluation reflect the interests of the ruling class and are by their very nature committed to obedience, inclusive militant religion is committed to the interest of classes seeking ascendancy. By an ascending class I mean those social classes whose members are conscious of their interest and are seeking to gain mobility in the class system.

The relationship between religious militancy and class has been observed by Engels and is articulated in his discussion of the peasant war in Germany. The first feature of this militancy is its emphasis on this world as opposed to an "other" world. From this religion's perspective, salvation is rooted in human interrelationships and only then with a relationship of a human to God. Reflecting the interest of the peasants, Münzer in his religious revolt saw heaven "not as a thing of another world . . . [I]t is the task of believers to establish this Heaven, the kingdom of God, here on earth. Just as there is no Heaven in the beyond . . . , there is no devil but man's lust and greed." The purpose of religion, at least this ascending class-based religion, is to establish God's kingdom on earth. By this kingdom, Münzer understood "a society in which there would be no class differences or private property and no state authority independent of or foreign to the members of society." Thus, "all work and all property" were to be "shared in common, and complete equality introduced."[14] Engels proposes two distinct qualities to be part of revolutionary religious doctrine: (1) it is to be this-world oriented, and (2) it should emphasize power responsibility and equality.

A this-worldly orientation of militant religion and its commitment to an ascending class was also observed more recently by Gary Marx. In examining the relationship between civil rights militancy and religion, he concluded that those religious individuals who have a temporal orientation are more likely to be committed to civil rights militancy than those who espouse an otherworldly orientation. Reviewing the data, he concludes "that an important factor in determining the effect of religion on protest attitudes is the nature of an individual's religious commitment. It is quite possible, for those with a temporal religious orientation, that . . . their religious concern serves to inspire and sustain race protest."[15] What is important to note is that the examples that Gary Marx cites (e.g., Martin Luther King, Jr.) are people who are conscious of their social class position and are seeking ascendancy.

Similarly the converse is also true. Rokeach reports that an otherworldly concern measured by a commitment to and a concern for personal salvation is negatively associated with a concern for civil rights and for the poor and was in opposition to the student protests of the 1960s.[16]

### Inclusive Militants and Values

Theology not only defines religious beliefs; it is also concerned with and defines moral values. These values, as Marx has indicated in his criticism of Feuerbach,[17] are not independent of the class positions of adherents. Thus, to understand the moral concerns associated with those religions that can be characterized as "inclusive militants" we need to understand their social class basis. Inclusive militants are by and large members of an ascending class— be they minorities, such as those in the civil rights movements of the 1960s, or the Liberation Theology groups of today. Gutiérrez, for instance, sees the new movement to be the church of the "erupting poor."[18] The religious moral values that are central to these militant religions reflect their members' social class and their quest for upward mobility. The three values that are central to persons in this position are justice, equality, and collectivity.

The values that are central in the Judeo-Christian tradition are justice and love. Of the two, it is justice that is most often associated with both political and religious liberalism.[19] Inclusive militants, whose political orientation is liberal, are thus more likely to espouse the ideals of justice rather than the more traditional Christian view of love. The religious conception of justice, particularly as it was defined by the Old Testament prophets, is a moral conception that defines the nature of the interpersonal relationship between two or more units in a social system who are in an asymmetrical power relationship. In the name of justice the prophets of the Old Testament, the militant leaders of their day, argue that the moral relationship between the poor and the mighty is one governed by equity. Injustice is the condition of exploitation. Justice exists when power relationships are governed by universally defined privileges and responsibilities that do not permit power abuse. The concern for justice now gives the articulators of Liberation Theology and other inclusive militant theologians a prophetic tone. Like the Old Testament prophets, particularly those who come from the lower class (e.g., Micah), like Mary in the Magnificat, the articulators of militant theology demand accountability of those in power, a concern for the poor and powerless.[20]

The second main value with which we are concerned, though in itself it may not have direct religious roots, is equality. Equality, in contrast to freedom, dominates the thinking of the lower class.[21] The idea of liberty, particularly as it developed in political discourses in the last century (e.g., J. S. Mill) stands in opposition to regulation and supports control by the powerful. Freedom, as conceptualized by Mill, serves best the interest of the powerful, rather than those seeking to improve conditions of social and economic ascendancy. It is equality that is thus central to the view of inclusive militant religious groups and their theology. Equality, not freedom, stands in alignment with the idea of justice—that is, against control by the powerful. It is equality that is antithetical to exploitation. Thus, a theology that seeks to support the rising poor in their struggle with their former exploiters is more likely to argue for equality, not only in the eyes of God in the hereafter, but as a temporal concern.

Together with justice, it becomes central to their conception of morality and to their temporal future.

The last value that is central to militant inclusivists and arises from their class concerns is a commitment to the collectivity. What is significant from this point of view is not individual salvation or the concern for the saving of the individual or the return of the prodigal son. Instead the commitment is to the group. All features of individualism, which in itself is the product of the Protestant marriage to capitalism, are rejected in favor of collective needs. Class interests are not individual interests; they are collective interests. This commitment in Christianity goes beyond the notion of *agapé*, but it is important as a means by which upward mobility for a whole class of people is demanded and justified. To face the power of the ruling class and oppose it, the ascending class needs to organize and present a united stand. It is only through collective action and voice that the power of the ruling class can be equaled by the ascending class.

### Exclusive Militant

Just as the inclusive militant religions reflect their class position so do the exclusive militants. Frequently these religions are perceived as the "militant right." In contrast to the universalist militant religions, those associated in and supporting militant exclusivism reflect concern for their *declining* status. The exclusivists differ from the inclusivists in that they seek to "return" to an earlier social and religious condition.[22] No doubt those who are part of this religious movement see the decline of a cherished culture, but they also see the economic and cultural basis of their earlier social status declining. In short they see the way of life in which, they believe, they held relatively higher status, in which their economic future was more assured because of their social position, a world in which their view and politics dominated, also declining. It is this feature of their existence that leads them to commit themselves to a religious view marked by both exclusivism and a past orientation.

The religious perspective of the retrenching class is thus one of sect-like characteristics. They are exclusive to the extent that they perceive religion—that is, one's view of God and what God wishes—

to be expressed by only one (their) theology. A commitment to retrenchment reflects a sense of conflict arising out of the threat of loss of position and their response to this threat, which usually consists of creating a fence around beliefs or worldview. In orthodox Judaism, for example, the idea is expressed in the dictum "to make a fence around the Torah"—i.e., not to permit an interpretation of the law that is counter to orthodoxy. Opposition to the world of modernity and to its new social order is achieved by rejecting the legitimacy of any other perspective that opens the world of ideas and morality to new meaning. Take for instance Falwell's statement: "[F]or America to stay free we must come back to the *only* principles that God can honor: the dignity of life, the traditional family, decency, morality and so on." But this can be achieved only through one religion; therefore it is his mission "to bring the nation back to a moral standard so that we can stay free in order that we can evangelize the world."[23]

Exclusivist militant religions are by and large past oriented. They see the world as paradise lost, and the mission of religion is to bring the world back to old values, to a world which "was." This orientation is well exemplified in the Hebrew word for penance— *t'shuvoh*—which actually means to return. Sin is moving away from an established mark. The central theme of the Christian right, Jewish orthodoxy, and militant Islam is "return"—not only to God, but also to a world that supposedly existed in the past, a moral world desired by God. As it also happens that-world-that-was is also the world in which values that supported these peoples' status were operative. Their honor and social position were determined by these values, and thus to return to them includes a return to the previous social order.

The basis of exclusivity lies not in equality. It does not seek to share with others, nor to change the system to one that supports the right of others to have equal claim or status and its prerogatives. It supports the ideals of the past, particularly those that have been incorporated into Protestantism: individualism, freedom, and love as the guiding principle of interpersonal association. Unlike the inclusivist, exclusivist militants stress individualism, which supports the right and legitimacy of differentiation and separation. The exclusivist, for example, does not see poverty to be inherent in the social order, but in the individual, his lack of commitment to work, and the absence of submission to God. Opposition to collective action on poverty and civil rights by religious conservatives has been clearly evident in Rokeach's work.[24] This commitment to individualism and the Protestant ethic is a value rooted in the past and has even been a part of the last century's "social gospel" movement. Individualism and freedom stand in diametric opposition to the liberal movements that seek change. The retrenching militant religion is opposed to modernity not only because it sees this lifestyle rejecting traditional religious values, but also because it rejects the basis of individual rights in asserting equality over freedom. Instead of equality, then, the exclusive militant groups will emphasize freedom. Freedom, like individualism, supports the legitimacy of class and property differences. The free individual has the right to amass goods and services. "Competition in business," Falwell says, "is Biblical. Ambitious and successful business management is clearly outlined as a part of God's plan for His people."[25] Competition and big business cannot exist unless they are supported by the "right" of individual freedom.

Commitment to the individual and opposition to class-based action against poverty is diametrically opposed to the ideal of justice in the prophetic sense. The exclusivists pervert justice into vengeance and retribution against individuals; they are opposed to it as the ideal that legitimates the curbing of the power of elites. Instead of justice, which is allied with equality, the militant advocates a one-sided love. Chandler, for instance, observes that "[T]he bellicose language of modern Fundamentalism is based on its paradoxical belief that aggression is the best expression of Christian love. ... Christ saw love as emanating from the strength of domination and power rather than from weakness and effeminacy."[26] But the importance of "love" to this theology as a whole is that it supports and accords with both individualism and freedom: Individuals are free to give or withhold love, whereas collectivities promote equality by establishing justice.

It is true that through love one is able to commiserate, empathize, and thus respond to the needs of others. Precisely because of this developed sense of empathy and concern, primary emphasis is placed on treating affected individuals rather than upon preventing problems in the first place. The most common activities of Christian missionaries, for instance, are feeding and healing. But help given to others for the sake of love lacks dependability; it is capricious because it must come as a "free will" or "love" offering. Because it leads us to be concerned with an individual and his or her problem, such love simultaneously detracts our attention from the social system as a whole, as well as from the concern for preventing problems—particularly if the solution to the problem lies in changing the social system. No clearer illustration of this plight can be seen than recent efforts to relieve hunger in Africa, which evinced great outpourings of love into systems so poorly designed (socially, economically, politically, technically) that it remains difficult to assess the benefits.

## CONCLUSION: JUSTICE AND MERCY

The commitment to "love," particularly as it is defined in Protestantism, is a legacy of the sociopolitical conditions of the early Christians, when access to effective political participation was essentially nil. But love, and all that it implies, enhances conservative ideology. In the name of Christian love, we place the burden of welfare on the individual and on the individual's emotional response. Love does not challenge the system that makes doing charity necessary in the first place. It is this value that characterizes submissive religions and is at once perverted and exalted by exclusive militarism. At most, love ties one individual to another; it demands no responsibility to or from the collective.

Justice, by contrast, is most often associated with social change. It is this value by which religions claim the right to reflect upon and criticize the ruling power. The problem that faces religion in the West is its overemphasis on the ideal of love—and, with it, "saving" individuals—rather than a commitment to justice and significant social and economic issues. Poverty and attendant social problems are moral issues that should not—and from a *sociological* point of view *cannot*—be relegated to the free will offerings of individuals. They are problems of *in*justice. If we love one another, we must thus seek justice for one another. Even more, however, true love is founded upon justice; so I read in *Bereshit Rabah*:

When God decided to create the world, He was contemplating whether He should create the world based on justice or on mercy. Were He to create the world only with justice, the Angels argued, who could withstand the purity and rigidity of that state alone. On the other hand, were He to create the world with only love and mercy, then no order would be possible. Therefore, He decided to create the world with justice tempered by mercy. Of the two thus justice is still considered to be the foundation of the social system.

# Part IV. APPLYING RELIGIOUS SOCIOLOGY

# 11. The Psychological Captivity of Evangelicalism

## Jack O. Balswick

If Freud were alive today he would find the "future of an illusion" (religion) to be more receptive of him than he was of it. Psychology is "in" within the evangelical community, as witnessed by the flood of psychologically oriented evangelical books available to the lay public. At many theological seminaries the fastest growing program is psychological counseling—whether expansion is considered in terms of new courses, additions to faculty, or student enrollments. Many ministers are spending more time counseling parishioners than preparing sermons. In casually thumbing through any of a number of Christian periodicals, one is struck by the multitude of psychologically oriented advertisements announcing seminars and workshops which promise increased psychological and spiritual wholeness to participants.

The purposes of this essay are to attempt to explain evangelicalism's preoccupation with psychology, the failure of evangelicalism to be informed by sociology, and the implications for evangelicalism of its psychological captivity. While some may find the ideas presented here presumptuous (and others nothing more than "sour grapes"), I will attempt to play the traditional ecclesiastical role of devil's advocate by forcefully delivering the ideas as sociological truths.

## THE FUNDAMENTALIST-MODERNIST CONTROVERSY

Any attempt to understand the evangelical preoccupation with psychology must begin with an understanding of the nature of the fundamentalist-modernist controversy which began in Germany in the late 1800s and found its way into every major American denomination by the early 1900s. The major issue in the controversy centered on what has come to be identified by fundamentalists and their descendents (i.e., evangelicals) as the "fundamentals of the faith." Fundamentalism began as a movement that attempted to preserve "historic" Christianity from the dual forces of modern scientific thought and modernism (i.e., liberal Christian theology). Fundamentalism, through an emphasis on the "fundamentals" of the faith (a belief in the virgin birth, miracles, the bodily resurrection of Christ, and the Bible as the inerrant, verbally inspired Word of God), developed into a movement that was built upon the negation of modernism as a theological approach to Christianity. Modernism, which held to the basic tenets that human beings are not sinful by nature and that utopia can be achieved on this earth merely by correcting evil social structures, was furthermore quite soundly shaken by two world wars and the great depression.

With the decline of modernism as a viable option, fundamentalism lost its foe and reason for being, while continuing its emphasis on negative ethics. Contained in this negative ethical set was a renunciation of things of the "world"—secular music, entertainment, cards, movies, alcoholic beverages, tobacco, and dancing. More important for our purposes, however, was the negation of secular wisdom, which showed itself in anti-intellectualism and suspicion of secular education with its reliance upon the scientific method. Fundamentalists emphasized the personal gospel, stressed humans' need for salvation, and almost totally neglected the social gospel, with its emphasis upon the need to change evil social structures.

The most salient controversy between fundamentalism and secular knowledge has centered upon the issue of creation versus evolution, supremely illustrated in the debate between Clarence Darrow and William Jennings Bryan at the celebrated Scopes "monkey trial." Fundamentalism's rejection of knowledge from the social and behavioral sciences was equally strong. A common argument against the need for psychotherapists was the belief that mental illness is a result of sin, and the necessary solution is a spiritual and not a psychological one.

## THE PSYCHOLOGICAL CAPTIVITY OF LIBERALISM

As fundamentalism's foe, liberalism was quick to accept knowledge from the natural sciences; it also found itself accepting the view of human nature contained within the emerging science of psychology of the 1920s and 1930s. The result was to reduce the traditional Biblical interpretation (which saw humans as sinful beings in need of salvation by a holy transcendent God) to a psychological interpretation of the human predicament. Within liberalism a simple "salvation" oriented Bible verse such as Acts 16:31— "Believe on the Lord Jesus Christ and thou shalt be saved"—came to be interpreted as meaning that by accepting the truths that Jesus taught (believe), one will be a whole person with an integrated personality (be saved).

In attempting to explain liberal Protestantism's acceptance of psychology, Vitz states that,

With the rise of secular ideas and values, especially psychological theories, the basic Christian concept of the unique importance of the self was stripped of its theological justification. Such traditional spiritual concepts as those which anchored the Christian self in experiences like prayer, contemplation, obedience, and mysticism—in faith—became so weak in mainline twentieth-century Protestantism as to be of little significance. The notion of pride as the fundamental sin—along with greed, envy, and the others— yielded to the belief that "the fundamental sin is to be chaotic and unfocused."[1]

The psychological captivity of liberalism can perhaps be best seen in the words of its leading preacher, Harry Emerson Fosdick, during its heyday of the 1920s to 1940s. Vitz summarizes Fosdick's position with quotes from his work:

To be a person is to be engaged in a perpetual process of becoming.... The basic urge of the human organism is toward wholeness. The primary command of our being is, Get yourself together, and the fundamental sin is to be chaotic and unfocused.... When at last maturity is reached..., the whole organism can be drawn together into that "acme of integration" which appears in creative work...in modern psychological parlance the word "integration" has taken the place of the religious word "Salvation."[2]

These quotations are taken from Fosdick's 1943 book, *On Being a Real Person*, and—ironically, perhaps—his work appears to have been prophetic of one of the directions that modern psychology has taken, as illustrated by Carl Rogers's more widely read book *On Becoming a Person*, authored twenty years later.

## THE EMERGENCE OF EVANGELICALISM

Although some are still fighting the modernist-fundamentalist battle, most of the ground captured in the modernist retreat of the 1940s and 1950s has been gained by an emerging new or neo-orthodoxy. Most mainline Protestant denominations and seminaries have been more influenced in the past fifty years by the writings of persons like Tillich, Bultmann, Niebuhr, Bonhoeffer, Brunner, and Barth than by the writings of old-time modernists or fundamentalists.

As the 1970s have given way to the 1980s, however, we find that the greatest growth in American Christianity has not been in liberalism, neo-orthodoxy, or fundamentalism, but in what has come to be called "evangelicalism." Richard Quebedeaux in his book *The Young Evangelicals* identifies evangelicalism as:

A school of Christianity which attests to the truth of three major theological principles: (1) the complete reliability and final authority of Scripture in matters of faith and practice; (2) the necessity of a *personal* faith in Jesus Christ as Savior from sin and consequent commitment to Him as Lord; and (3) the urgency of seeking actively the conversion of sinners to Christ.[3]

The early strength of the evangelical resurgence began to be documented in the early 1970s. Dean Kelley, in his 1972 book, *Why Conservative Churches Are Growing*, documented the spectacular growth of evangelical churches. Kelley hypothesized that these churches were growing because, unlike liberal churches, they were providing clear answers to people's questions concerning the ultimate purpose and meaning of life. In his book, which he provocatively entitled *The Evangelical Renaissance*, David Bloesch devotes his first chapter to documenting the growth of the evangelical perspective in Protestant denominations, the Roman Catholic Church, college campus organizations, television and radio broadcasting, book publishing, Christian magazines and periodicals, seminaries and Bible colleges, and a multitude of extradenominational fellowships, communities, and renewal movements. Evidence for the continued growth in evangelicalism can be seen in the "born again" emphasis of the late 1970s. In 1984, the leading poll-taker in the United States, George Gallup, reported that forty percent of all Americans consider themselves "born again" Christians.[4]

What distinguishes evangelicalism in its present appearance (which was first referred to as "the new evangelicalism" or "neo-evangelicalism") is a willingness to put away much of the negativism which was a part of earlier fundamentalism. This includes negativism toward the "things of the world,"[5] and toward secular and scientific knowledge.[6] The theological content of fundamentalism (the "fundamentals of the faith") continue to be held intact. Although there has been some attempt by evangelicals to grapple with the social implications of the gospel, the "gospel" for the most part continues to be interpreted in an individual way.

The distinction between evangelicalism and fundamentalism can better be made on sociological rather than theological grounds. Those who continue to be a part of fundamentalism are largely concentrated in the lower socio-economic class. They are a part of what H. Richard Niebuhr referred to as the "church of the disinherited" and constitute sectarian religion.[7] From the point of view of an early "new evangelical" theologian, fundamentalism is "orthodoxy gone cultic."[8]

One of the characteristics of sectarian religion is that members are converted into it rather than born into it. The route for many who were born into fundamentalism was to achieve higher social status than that into which they were born and to undergo a resultant change in religious style. There are few second or third generation fundamentalists, for those who "keep the faith" are most likely to wind up middle class and evangelical. Not surprisingly from this perspective, evangelicalism is almost exclusively a middle- and upper-middle-class religion. For the most part it is their "disinherited" brothers and sisters who are fighting the old modernist-fundamentalist battles anew. Evangelicals themselves have become "enlightened" by the wisdom and usefulness of secular knowledge. They value education, the American way of life, and are among the strongest defenders of the American middle-class lifestyle.

Increasingly, what has become the core image of human being in the great American middle-class lifestyle is a psychological view toward life. There exists within evangelicalism an individualistic emphasis, which has roots going back to fundamentalism, which makes evangelicalism highly susceptible to the emergent "psychological society." Martin Gross, in his book *The Psychological Society*, argues that, in the United States, psychology and the psychological expert have come to be the new "scientific" standard of behavior, replacing the Protestant ethic, which has weakened and is gradually fading from the American scene. Although Gross has greatly overestimated the demise of the Judeo-Christian religion as a basis that Americans can use as a standard of behavior, there is an element of truth in his thesis. As a society we have become a people who place a psychological interpretation on all events in our lives. What I think Gross has failed to see is the extent to which Christian believers have held onto their Christianity by letting it become psychologized.

## THE PSYCHOLIZATION OF EVANGELICALISM

Broadly speaking (and admittedly overgeneralizing), there are two approaches that can be used in attempting to bring about desired social change. First, an attempt can be made to change individuals, with the expectation that once individuals have become changed persons they will then bring about needed changes in social structures. Second, an attempt can be made to change social structures, with the expectation that once social structures are changed the lives of the persons who participate within them will change. The fundamentalist-modernist controversy can be understood in large part as an argument over the perfect way of implementing change. Fundamentalists opted for changing individuals, while modernists opted for changing social structures. These contrasting emphases came to be known as the personal gospel and the social gospel, respectively.

By increasingly recognizing the legitimate social implications of the gospel, evangelicals are decreasingly caught up in an emphasis upon the personal gospel at the neglect of the social gospel. The social conscience of evangelicals has become increasingly sensitized to needed social change. However, there is within evangelicalism a carry-over of an individual emphasis which has its roots in the fundamentalist rejection of the social gospel. While evangelicals recognize the need for social change, they still believe that the most effective means of bringing about that change is to deal with individuals and not social structures. Substitute *Christian counseling* for *personal salvation* and *social reconstruction* for *social gospel*, and we have the fundamentalist-modernist controversy in modern dress. This is certainly not to say that evangelicals do not believe in personal salvation. They do! But, in contrast to earlier fundamentalists, they no longer believe that personal salvation or conversion will bring about a totally changed person—morally, socially, and psychologically. Evangelicals now recognize that it is too simple an answer to believe that all personal and social problems will dissipate when one "turns to Jesus." Rather, the educationally enlightened evangelical recognizes the benefit of counseling and psychotherapy to the "saved" and "unsaved" alike.

The model of change employed within evangelicalism is this: (1) Actively seek the conversion of sinners to Christ. (2) Utilize the best principles of counseling and psychotherapy to allow persons to become more fully healed (whole, *salus*). And (3), wait for the resultant change in social structures as these regenerated whole persons live their Christianity in society. Under certain circumstances, furthermore, the first and second steps can be reversed. This is especially thought to be necessary when an individual is so psychologically disturbed as to prevent that individual from actually hearing and acting upon the "good news" of the gospel. Evangelicals also stress that the hearing of the gospel is facilitated by the hearers having full rather than empty stomachs (an old controversy from the foreign mission field as well). This is to say that evangelicals are very attuned to meeting the social needs of the unconverted either before or simultaneously with the presentation of the gospel.

Evangelicals are concerned about the social, racial, and political problems of society and actively want to participate in the elimination of these problems. For the most part, however, they believe that the best solution to these societal problems is the conversion of individuals to Jesus Christ. A good illustration of this view can be seen in the statements of Dr. Bill Bright, the founder and president of Campus Crusade for Christ, the largest and most active evangelical college student ministry in the world. Bright states that, "There is no political structure, no social problem, no personal need anywhere for which Christ is not the answer." Or again, "The world can be changed only as men's lives are changed. Jesus Christ is the one person who can change a man from within, who can give meaning, purpose, and direction to men's lives." Or finally, "It is not misleading to suggest that our twentieth century world can be changed in the same sense that the first century world was turned upside down. When individuals are changed in sufficient numbers, homes and communities will be changed. Cities, states, and nations of the world will feel the impact of the transformed lives of the men and women who have been introduced to Jesus Christ."[9] At Expo 72, Bright made the statement, "Expo 72 can do more to bring peace to the world than all of the antiwar activity we have been seeing. Changed people in sufficient numbers make a changed world."[10]

It is the psychological captivity of evangelicalism that prevents it from seeing the naïveté in its assumption that changed individuals will automatically bring about changed social structures. Psychological blinders prevent evangelicals from being informed or enlightened by a sociological view of reality that would demonstrate that individuals are not only shaped by social structures, but also *maintained* by social structures.[11] To concentrate on changing the individual, as opposed to the social structure, can be very inefficient when these "changed" individuals are returned to the social conditions that were partly responsible for creating and reinforcing their former selves.

## PREVENTION AND TREATMENT WITHIN EVANGELICALISM

One result of the psychological captivity of evangelicalism is that in a social and psychological sense it concentrates upon treatment rather than prevention. There is a case to be made, however, that in a theological sense evangelicalism, by stressing the need for individual regeneration deals more with prevention than liberalism does—the latter does not see humans as in need of regeneration and, hence, directs most of its effort to propping up social structures that fallen human beings keep perverting. Rather, the point to be made here is that individual counseling has the effect of changing the individual who is in need, but does very little about changing the social structures that most contribute to the problems of the individual. Another way of putting it is to say that alcoholism, mental distress, marital conflict, rebellious children, and the like are merely symptoms of deeper problems that are built into the social structure of American—or any—society. This is the important distinction that Peter Berger makes between social problems and sociological problems.[12] When the troubled person is counseled, it is the symptom and not the cause of the problem that is being dealt with. I am not arguing that counseling should not be done as a part of a Christian responsibility to a broken world, but that Christian responsibility to a broken *world* does not stop here. A part of the Christian response to a broken world should also be an attempt to change the alienating, evil, dehumanizing, or sinful social *structures* which are *producing* alcoholism, mental distress, marital difficulties, or rebellious children.

As an example of what I mean by needed social structural change, consider the societal factors that might contribute to marital breakdown. By taking an individual (psychological) perspective, we might argue that marital difficulties are a result of immaturity on the part of one or both of the persons involved in the marriage. Although personal maturity is very important in marriage, there are also a number of societal factors that contribute to marital difficulties in modern society. One would be the impersonal and bureaucratic nature of the work-a-day world. The husband or wife who ventures into this world to work feels various social pressures that can affect the marital relationship. The current redefinition of sex roles is another factor that can affect a marriage. American society is currently undergoing a redefinition of what it means to be a man and what it means to be a woman. Marital adjustment is not the easiest thing to accomplish when one is questioning the basis of one's sexuality, to say nothing of the whole process of questioning traditional ways of dividing marital tasks—earning money, cooking, cleaning, caring for the children, making decisions, and the like. These and numerous other societal factors are having an effect upon marriage in the contemporary Western world.

## ACTIONS, ATTITUDES, AND EVANGELICALS

Another result of the psychological captivity of evangelicalism is that evangelicals tend to concentrate on changing attitudes rather than actions. This was especially evident in the resistance within the evangelical community to any attempt on the part of government to "force" change in the civil rights struggle for justice and equal participation in American society. It tends to continue to manifest itself in reaction to racial tensions in South Africa. Even if one is willing to grant that most evangelicals are *not* racially prejudiced people, one will still find them resistant to any attempt to bring about change by even legitimate force; legislation is thought to be unable to change the "hearts" of human beings. It is argued that people discriminate because they are prejudiced, and logic therefore dictates that racism will be eliminated by concentrating on the reduction of prejudice. To attempt the reduction of prejudice is, of course, to concentrate on changing attitudes, while attempting to reduce discrimination is to take action. The psycholization of evangelicalism results in evangelicals interpreting the Bible in ways that lead them to attempt to change people from "within," rather than attempting to "force" change from without.

There are three ironies in the position evangelicals take on the relationship between attitudes and actions.

The first is that much of the early theorizing and research relevant to the logic of attempting to change discrimination rather than prejudice was done by a psychologist. It was Gordon Allport who first suggested that attempting to change people's "hearts" is infinitely less effective than forcing them to change their actions by changing the *social structures* that permit discrimination.[13] The whole intellectual underpinning for the strategy of social change in the American civil rights movement is founded on Allport's and others' findings that although racism can be reduced very little by focusing upon prejudice, it can be effectively reduced by forcing change in behavior through the modification of laws, social institutions, and related social structures.

The second irony is that when evangelicals do advance a legislative agenda, it tends so to dissociate action from attitude, and individuals from social structures, as to be almost impossible to enforce in practice. Anti-alcohol, anti-abortion, anti-pornography as evangelical social issues tend ultimately to be unsuccessful because, while attempting merely to prohibit specific actions, they do not recognize the intimate connection between social structure, actions, and attitudes.

The final irony has to do with their selective *inattention* to Jesus's statement, "Where your money is, there shall your heart be also." It is manifest here that Jesus is teaching that commitments (actions) determine attitudes. Understanding the implications of such statements might be a rich source for the development of a new view of social change within evangelicalism.

## CONCLUSIONS

It is *not* academic psychology that evangelicalism embraces to a greater extent than sociology. There is very little difference between the views of the majority of psychologists and sociologists on the importance of the *social context* of behavioral origin, maintenance, and change. Evangelicalism has been captured by psychologism in a narrower sense; namely, a very individualistic view of action, especially of the changing of action patterns.

Evangelicals claim to be concerned with the full application of the Christian gospel and to be open to the truths gleaned by all aspects of the scientific enterprise. If they are to be true to their claims, they should be willing to be informed by sociology more than is presently the case. If sociological insights are accepted, evangelicals will realize a Christian responsibility to deal with individuals *and* social structures.

Some evangelicals are attempting to present a more complete model of Christian responsibility. The most notable examples are the periodicals *Sojourners* and *The Other Side*, and books such as David Moberg's *The Great Reversal*, Richard Mouw's *Political Evangelism*, and Ronald Sider's *Rich Christians in an Age of Hunger*. However, those who speak for concerted efforts to change social structures are still rather lonely and somewhat suspect voices in evangelical circles.[14] Although any academically respectable evangelical seminary will have a resident *clinical* psychologist or two, not to mention professors of "pastoral counseling" in abundance, it is hard to think of more than one that includes a single full-time sociologist. If any change is to take place, I predict it will not originate from evangelical seminaries, but rather from the growing numbers of evangelical sociologists who are teaching and writing at both Christian and secular colleges and universities.

Given evangelical's firm reliance upon Biblical authority and their fear of theological liberalism, resistance to sociological input will come in the form of theological justifications. The origin of this fear will be in evangelicalism's memory of the "unholy" alliance of theological liberalism and Christian sociology at the turn of this century. It is almost as if evangelicals possess a "collective unconscious"[15] which dictates that they will tenaciously hold on to an individualistic understanding of the Christian gospel.

# 12. Clinical Pastoral Sociology

## William H. Swatos, Jr.

As Jack Balswick has noted, pastoral psychology has enjoyed considerable popularity in American churches, frequently defining an essential role-performance of a "professional" minister. Sociology, by contrast, has often been regarded as suspect and identified simplistically with social action. To some extent this merely mirrors trends in the dominant culture. Other reasons may lie in Protestant theology's emphasis upon individual salvation or in sociology's tendency until very recently to remain aloof from application. Regardless of the background factors, here as in many other applied areas, sociologists have largely been "certified out" of the field. A sociologist who is also an ordained functionary of a religious body, and who combines these sets of expertise to address the problems individuals face within the social relationships of their lives, will find it difficult to put these competencies to work in ways that either peers or potential clients will recognize as valuable. "Clinical pastoral education," the formal name and structure under which pastoral psychology has been institutionalized, has created a self-perpetuating certification and accrediting system in which sociological theory and training finds little place.[1] Yet pastoral counselors are ready not only to practice their profession in the churches but to market their services to a wider public as well.[2]

Clinical pastoral sociology as I envision it is clinical sociology applied within the specific context of the religious institution and the pastor-congregant role relationship. This may occur either in the local church or in a religious counseling center. Clinical pastoral *sociology* differs from traditional "pastoral counseling" in that it emphasizes the web of social interaction—including divine-human interaction as a form of social interaction—rather than the individual standing relatively alone vis-á-vis both divinity and society. Clinical *pastoral* sociology also differs from clinical sociology, however, inasmuch as it accepts and builds upon assumptions about the reality of revealed religion. It is sociology applied within a shared structure of religious value and meaning. Within Christianity, for example, clinical pastoral sociology can affirm that God is not a *deus solitarius* but a *deus triunus*, that the Godhead itself is persons-in-relationship and that humanity is created in this interpersonal image. Sin is the breaking of the image—imperfect relationships. Again, we are told in the Incarnation that the *Word* became flesh; language as constitutive of humanity can be explored in unique ways by those with sociological expertise. The importance of the charismatic band to the mission of the charismatic leader, noted by Weber,[3] is another salient theological theme. A Christian doing clinical pastoral sociology uses these themes along with sociological theory to counsel the client in ways that would not necessarily be appropriate to a secular context. Other religious traditions would do the same, emphasizing their own salient stories.

As clinical pastoral sociology addresses aspects of clients' lives that relate to pragmatic experiential questions (e.g., how to proceed in a divorce settlement), the practice is likely to verge more closely to that of clinical sociology *sans phrase*. As questions about the client's relationship to deity are raised, the approach will take a more theological turn. The important point in either case, however, is that regardless of the theological or pragmatic valence attached to a given application, the theoretical structure is fundamentally sociological: *social* variables are given explanatory priority. Not "One Solitary Life," but "Living the Charismatic Relationship" is the basic theme.[4]

## REDUCTIONISM AND RELIGION

Some styles of both psychology and sociology have reduced the possibility of religious truth to nothing. At this extreme religion becomes "only" the projection—usually "unconscious"—of some empirical state, value, or wish by an individual or group into a suprahuman mode in order to achieve specific ends—also usually "unconscious." Reductionist psychologists tend to see this activity as potentially negative or actually harmful to the wellbeing of the client. Sociologists tend to be more mixed in their reaction. Functionalists see religion as essential to social stability; Marxists, more like the psychologists, see it as obfuscating "real" conditions. Little pastoral psychology is as reductionistic as the postures characterized here. Within the context of ministerial training, however, there are strong pressures toward "humanistic" professionalism,[5] and products of this education may often articulate their role in terms of disabusing rank-and-file congregants of outmoded theological notions.[6]

Many pastoral psychologists—particularly within the more evangelical churches—are able to integrate their work with traditional theological categories. California's Fuller Theological Seminary, a flagship school for the evangelical movement, offers a graduate clinical psychology degree to students whose religious orientation is likely to be far from Garrett Seminary's humanistic professionals. Yet within pastoral psychology the seeds of religion's own destruction are sown. By emphasizing the "troubled individual," pastoral psychology enhances the individuation, atomization, and secularization of modernity. Today's typical pastoral counselor is the extension of a process of religious privatization that has been going on for centuries. Religious categories become particular therapeutic modalities by means of which individuals cope with the "world." Thus, even in its least reductionistic posture, pastoral psychology reduces religion to a *socially meaningless* category. Religion is not a system of interaction but an "alternate healing system" for individuals. Perhaps Marx said more than he intended when he referred to religion as the "opiate of the people."

The origins of "clinical pastoral education" can be traced to the Flexner Report on medical education sponsored by the Carnegie Foundation early in this century. Although the policy of the separation of church and state delayed the speed of reaction in the professional training of ministers as contrasted with physicians, there was a very conscious effort from 1924 onwards to adopt and implement the medical model for professional ministerial education and practice.[7] Central to this process was the work of Anton Boisen, himself a psychiatric patient and minister. Influenced by psychologist Richard Cabot, Boisen introduced a program in 1925 to foster "cooperative inquiry" between physicians and ministers, "into the psychology of religious experience,"[8] and by 1930 the Council for the Clinical Training of Theological Students had been formed.[9] Boisen's own book, *Out of the Depths: An Autobiographical Study of Mental Disorder and Religious Experience*, is both emblematic and symptomatic of the underlying crisis-orientation that characterizes pastoral psychology.[10] Boisen saw a kinship between mental illness and religious experience as "problem solving" techniques in an individual's life. Thus the minister should be trained "in the art of helping people out of trouble and enabling them to find spiritual health."[11] An association between religion and sickness or "un-wellness" runs through this literature, as does the role of the minister as healing professional.

The medical model for pastoral psychology is not merely metaphoric. Almost all clinical pastoral education (CPE) takes place in hospital settings. This reinforces the association between illness, institutionalization, individuation, and religion. Sick individuals are put into treatment institutions where a technique is employed by virtue of which (if successful) they are able to rejoin society. Medical sociologists, of course, have recognized the importance of social factors in the etiology of both physical and mental illness for decades; the implementation of this knowledge is another question. From the viewpoint of the sociology of institutions and sociological problems as contrasted with social problems, however, the confusion of religion and medicine as spheres of social life in the CPE model is obvious.

In addition to the psychological reduction of religion to a socially meaningless category perpetrated by pastoral psychology, this therapeutic mode serves to legitimize the existing social system. The individual is enabled to "cope" with society; society is unquestioned:

The source, if not the cause, of mental disorders is invariably traced to the client himself and/or his friends and relations. Society-at-large does not, and cannot, figure significantly in these treatments, although the collective ill-effects of living day-to-day in advanced industrial society have been repeatedly demonstrated. Thus psychology, counseling, and allied techniques further privatize the individual, leading her or him to search for exclusively existential solutions, more sophisticated avoidance mechanisms, and tried and true adjustment techniques. Marcuse's remark about "shrinks" being so-called because they shrink minds to manageable proportions is appropriate as social problems are telescoped into personal ones.[12]

More than any previous modality of religious institutional expression, pastoral psychology serves to make the religious institution a tool of the secular system of power in society.

The sociological reduction of religion in the Durkheimian and Marxist formulations, however, also constitutes a problem for clinical pastoral sociology, but only if we accept these paradigms as definitive for religion. Although each is widely held, neither is unproblematic nor fully sustained by empirical evidence. This is not the place for a full discussion of the definition question in the sociology of religion.[13] Elsewhere, I have suggested an alternative non-reductionist approach to religion based upon W. I. Thomas's concept of the "definition of the situation."[14] This proposition—perhaps as close to a law as any theoretical statement sociology has to offer—holds, simply, that a situation is what it is defined to be by its participants and that any aspect of social life is "real," if it is real in its consequences. The definition is thus a process of action prior to abstraction. It is lived in experience prior to being articulated in a definition. Using this approach to reach the underlying meaning codes which enable us to define religion, we must examine the processes by which participants in the action system know themselves or others to be engaging in religious action. Religion is defined here simply as how people relate to what they consider to be supraempirical, supernatural, transcendent realities. Any aspect of human action dealing with this category of experience is thus included. Action without this reference is excluded. Definitions and their alterations develop out of interaction, not *a priori*. An interpretive context on the part of the participants determines the significance of the action.

A situational approach to religion overcomes all the reductionist tendencies inherent in some other sociological approaches, while at the same time being squarely centered in well-founded and tested sociological theory. It is "heretical" in that it abandons some taken-for-granted orthodoxies within the field; yet it is entirely unclear what these belief-like propositions are doing in a scientific discipline anyway. With an irony that Weber might have most appreciated, a rejection of doctrinaire functionalist statements about religion (Marx's position included), enables us to take religion seriously as an action system within a sociological framework of analysis which has proved eminently viable for handling a wide variety of forms of social life. In particular, the situational approach frees clinical pastoral sociology from the medical model inasmuch as the possibility for a "real" religious definition of a situation grants institutional independence to religion and its practitioners.

## THE PROFESSION OF MINISTRY

In a historical survey of New England church life, Scott has traced the move in the ministry *From Office to Profession* from 1750 to 1850. Although his end date may be a bit early, the development of a professional model of ministry based on criteria of technical rationality was in full swing by the early twentieth century.[15] Yet it is difficult to discern in exactly what ways the modern "professional" minister is a professional.[16] Clearly the modern minister is not the medieval priest, with a monopoly on the dispensation of God's grace. Yet Freidson notes that in order to maintain its authority, a professional group must exercise a monopoly over a specific body of knowledge, whose practice it then licenses.[17] The ministry is clearly non-exclusive, inasmuch as denominational pluralism practically guarantees the non-professional character of the ministry. Not only do criteria for ordination vary considerably among denominations, but it is also possible to be an ecclesiastical entrepreneur —to found one's "own" church. A rising interest in "lay ministries" in practically every denomination, furthermore, has largely undermined the unique functions of the "professional" minister within the narrower walls of a specific faith tradition. Likewise, if the minister poses as a "humanistic professional," competition is close at hand from other agents and agencies. There is, then, a question of just what it is that makes the minister a minister. Ministerial self-definition may become a matter of the origin of a paycheck. If the minister is a "healing professional," the hegemony of the medical model largely trivializes his or her function.

Clinical pastoral sociology using a situational approach to religion, by contrast, recognizes the religious professional as a *religious professional*—the *sui generis* character of religion as an action system in which human beings freely participate gives an institutional framework within which the minister participates. This does not mean either that all ministers are sociologists or all sociologists ministers. What it does mean is that a religious worldview can be taken seriously on its own terms and yet employ sociological theory in problem assessment. Rather than reducing religion to a private sphere of attitude adjustment, a situationalist approach permits the pastor to take religion seriously in understanding the interaction patterns that cause the client to be in a particular situation or express a given need in a given situation. The task of the clinical pastoral sociologist, then, is to engage with the client in an operation *verstehen* by means of which an interpretive context for action is established and alternative interpretations brought into perspective. Situations, rather than pathologies, become the central concern, and "What is going on here in terms of social interaction and what does it mean?" the central questions.

In a recent work on how professionals actually function in performance settings, Schön has suggested a method which he terms "reflection in action." While his emphasis on the uniqueness of individual cases may initially seem unsatisfactory to sociologists, his underlying model is situational. His suggestion that professional practice is an "art" has been presaged in sociology, for example, by Nisbet.[18] Specifically, he argues that rather than the model of technical rationality providing a predefined technical solution to a problem, the professional develops a unique "artistic" solution to fit the situation: "His artistry is evident in his selective management of large amounts of information, his ability to spin out long lines of invention and inference, and his capacity to hold several ways of looking at things at once without disrupting the flow of inquiry."[19] A clinical pastoral sociologist, then, takes the science of sociology as well as the science of theology and shapes both artistically in application to specific situations. That a situation is defined as religious by its participants creates a reality-context within which problem solving becomes meaningful. If there is any "therapy" going on, it is "therapeutic" of the situation (in the phenomenological sense), not of the individual.

## PRACTICAL APPLICATIONS

Inherent in the situationalism I am advocating is a rejection of certain problem-types and solutions. At the same time, I want to make it quite clear that I am not suggesting an "anything goes" approach to pastoral work under the guise of sociology. Rather, I am arguing for a method that takes the internal logics of religion seriously, while at the same time recognizing that specific individuals will bring unique interaction sets to the counselor that preclude an *a priori* "diagnosis." I also do not want to deny that there are persons who are genuinely mentally ill or that religion may be either cause or symptom of illness.[20] A person who is both theologically trained and sociologically sophisticated ought to be able to discern relatively easily whether or not a specific client is amenable to a moderately sustained, rational conversation about his or her situation. My point, drawn from over a decade of counseling experience, is that most people who seek a religious professional are capable of such dialogue and expect to have religious needs and expressions taken seriously.

The dominant psychological model—both in religion and elsewhere—does not lead people, however, to anticipate an interactive model. People bring "my problem" or sometimes with a spouse or child "his or her problem." I must begin, then, to lead the client in the direction of seeing a "problem situation," and in all likelihood of seeing that problem situation as an outgrowth of prior problem situations. Two things often happen almost simultaneously at this point. One is a certain degree of relief as some anxiety is displaced onto a wider sphere of relationships. One no longer has a problem by oneself. Concurrently, however, a degree of frustration sets in as it frequently seems far more difficult to change a situation than to "cure" a disease. Some clients prefer the medical model, it seems, precisely because it treats symptoms. But sometimes breakthroughs do occur.

In divorce counseling, for example, I consider that we have made great progress whenever one party comes to the point of recognizing that each of the twosome has a different view of an event or issue, both of which are equally "real," neither of which is necessarily right or wrong. The recognition that different circumstances can give different perspectives on the same event begins to open up the possibility for genuine dialogue, not necessarily reconciliation in the traditional sense. At the same time, however, this can encourage reflection upon the meaning of reconciliation not only in the immediate context of the marriage, but also in a larger theological and sociological context. The fallibility of specific structures can be thrown into relief against larger meanings. We can then speculate on why marriage seems—*socio-structurally*—so"easy and natural" at the time it is entered into, but so difficult afterwards. Decisions about premarital pregnancy, abortion, the "right things to do," parent-child relationships, and the like are open to discussion not in terms of abstract principles but of interactions and situations. This is not, however, the simplistic "situation ethics" of the 1960s, which largely ignored such factors as historicity and control,[21] but a recognition of the persistence of socio-cultural forms, often across multiple generations. This approach also gives a concrete social-experiential understanding, not a vague reference to "human nature."

Taking religion seriously also permits questions of death and dying to be addressed in a more open and frank manner than a typical "therapeutic" mentality allows. Frequently the concerns that are raised in such encounters move back and forth between matters of extreme ultimacy—"What is heaven like?"—to much more mundane, but not necessarily less important or non-theological, issues—such as the decision for cremation versus burial, the appropriateness of organ transplants, or the use of incense during the burial liturgy. Socio-cultural, economic, theological, and psychological considerations interact in a complex web of relationships that do not permit simple solutions. Likewise, the wishes of the deceased may be honored scrupulously or ignored almost totally for a whole series of reasons which in turn rest upon both historical and contemporary factors that are not easily reduced to any particular calculus. Clinical pastoral sociology as reflective action provides an orientation, but not a technique, to the "ecclesial person" for assessing a situation and moving toward a resolution.[22] Any preordained decision—e.g., "Always follow the wishes of the deceased"—is doomed to failure, whereas spinning out lines of invention and inference is likely to lead to positive results. A Weberian consciousness of the constant dialectic in the personality between rational and irrational elements can contribute much here, as can an awareness of the constantly ongoing process of socialization.

As a priest, I have become increasingly sensitive to the possibility that the jokes that compare weddings to funerals may also reflect more about social processes than their humor first displays. As sociologists, of course, we often talk in rather dispassionate terms about various rites of passage, and both church members and sociologists are intrigued by those who set foot in the place only for these rites. But in addition there is something fundamentally *de*-stabilizing about modern weddings, just as there is about a funeral. This liminal situation is charged with mixed valences. The formal ritual provides only a thin veneer under which a variety of conflicting motives, expectations, and interaction patterns play upon each other. To say this is not merely to highlight the reality of "informal wedding rituals," which of course are also present and which may well outweigh the formal ceremony in importance to the participants. The wedding ends a period of life that is increasingly celebrated as itself the quintessence of human existence; whereas marriage becomes a purgatory for old age. The numeric and proportional increase of representatives of "failed" marriages in attendance at weddings gives very different signals from the strong communal ties into which a couple was once integrated. We do not have to wax romantic on yesteryear to recognize that the symbolic significance of the wedding has markedly altered. Again, the psychological emphasis of much premarital counseling—"What are your needs and how will marriage meet them for you?"—has only further served to deemphasize marriage as an event of societal importance.

I have already discussed the importance of prayer to religion and the inadequacy of sociological attention to this topic. My own focus has been primarily on power relationships in the practice of prayer. George Hillery, by contrast, has noted the importance of an association between prayer and love. Perhaps these two can be merged into a theory of freedom and control or used to understand more clearly what kinds of interaction patterns are involved in that elusive relationship we call "love." At the level of application, specifically, the situational approach takes prayer as real in itself. We have no need to try to explain prayer away. Rather, we take prayer as data for analysis and people praying as human beings engaged in social action. In clinical *pastoral* sociology, however, we also can make the "leap of faith" to *inter*action. We not only posit deity in order to give meaning to the encounter; we also affirm the relationship between the participants in the action system. From this, the most basic pastoral function, spiritual direction, becomes a legitimate identity for the practitioner. The clinical pastoral sociologist does not attempt to make everyday life meaningful by finding an extra-terrestrial "therapy," but rather by understanding and interpreting the everyday life of the believer in terms of a system of interaction across multiple levels of "reality."

In this way, the ministry is freed from the "crisis" setting of attempting to exercise a monopoly over a technical-rational sphere of unique competence—which it never could do anyway without fundamentally contradicting itself—to being a reflective-critical art based upon personal competence. The medical model can be totally discarded. In its place artistry comes to the fore. Clinical pastoral sociology is *not a technique but a "way of seeing,"* a true herme-neutic that balances charismatic freedom with the concerns of the community.[23] The clinical pastoral sociologist offers an interpretive framework for interaction rooted in the possibility that deity is real.

## INDUCTIVE THEOLOGY

In *The Heretical Imperative* (a somewhat misleading title), Peter Berger issues a call for a theology that consciously issues from human experience.[24] A thoroughly sociological historical-critical approach would insist that this is what theology always has been, though perhaps "unconsciously," and mechanisms of reification notwithstanding. Creative developments in the sociology of religion such as those by Richard Quinney and Edward Bailey, much of which still remain unpublished,[25] likewise move in rather contro-versial ways beyond the analysis of religion to religious "theory construction"—i.e., theology. The central thrust of these works is to take religious experience seriously as human experience, on the one hand, while on the other formulating a concept of deity based upon these empirical data. That what comes out may sound more like poetry than either theology or sociology merely evinces the artistic quality of reflective practice as against the assumptions of technical rationality, which are in fact largely based upon a *deductive* model for both science and religion. Kuhn has seriously challenged the simplistic quality of this method-in-practice in the natural sciences;[26] perhaps a recognition of this fallacy-in-practice might restore theology to a legitimate place among the human sciences.

Central to the task of the clinical pastoral sociologist, then, is the process of enabling the client to define the deity-human interaction pattern. This is not a Bible-quiz or an exercise in scholasticism. It is rather in the nature of questions such as these: "If you say this about your neighbor, what does it say about God?," and "If you say this about God, what does it say about your neighbor?" What I am urging is not a simplistic negation of historic revelation, but the possibility of giving meaning to that corpus through experience. John Maynard Keynes reminded us half a century ago, as if we didn't know it already, that in the long run we will all be dead; yet we perceive in the bulk of human beings a tremendous desire to live. How we deal with that paradox is the basis of all theology. Inasmuch as it is a shared predicament, it is a sociological problem—and one of global significance. Transcending and mediating the aloneness of the extinction of individual existence and the continuation of the world is the art of ministry. The vision of hope or despair that is pictured has real consequences for how we will live our lives in the short run, and most religions have suggested that this is the race that matters in the long run.

# Notes

## PREFACE

1. For example, Lyon, 1976; DeSanto et al., 1980; DeSanto and Poloma, 1985; Gaede, 1985; also see Poloma, 1982; Cavanaugh, 1982. The tendency is not limited to Christianity; on Buddhist sociology, see, e.g., Bell, 1979.

2. Anthony Campolo's *A Reasonable Faith*; see Moberg, 1986.

3. See Coste, 1985.

4. See, e.g., Hadden and Shupe, 1986; Moss, 1986; Planas, 1986.

5. In Desroche, 1973: viii; see also, Husserl, 1970; Pannenburg, 1976.

6. But see Peacocke, 1981.

7. Swatos, 1984b; see Wallis and Bruce, 1986.

8. E.g., Vidich and Lyman, 1985; Dynes, 1974.

9. See Swatos, 1977, 1984a.

10. I don't know whether she invented it, but I owe this felicitous phrase to Ruth Cavan (see Cavan, 1983: 409).

11. Berger, 1969: 40: "Once we know that all human affirmations are subject to scientifically graspable socio-historical processes, *which affirmations are true and which are false?* We cannot avoid the question any more than we can return to the innocence of its pre-relativizing asking."

12. See Swatos, 1980. I am indebted to Gert Mueller for pointing out to me the importance of "faith" or "trust" in the definition of religion (see Mueller, 1980).

13. See Swatos, 1980; Barth, 1961: 117.

14. Wittgenstein, 1958: 1.

15. So, e.g., the Athanasian Symbol.

16. Hillery, 1982.

17. Swatos, 1984b.

## 1. FAITH, FACTS, AND VALUES IN THE SOCIOLOGY OF RELIGION

1. Friedrichs, 1974.
2. See, e.g., Anthony, 1982; Anthony and Robbins, 1975; Anthony et al., 1974; Bellah, 1970, 1975; Berger, 1967, 1969, 1974; Berger and Neuhaus, 1976; Fichter, 1972; Friedrichs, 1974; Garrett, 1974; Glock, 1972, 1976; Glock and Stark, 1965; Robbins et al., 1973.
3. See also Swatos, 1984b.
4. Parsons, 1937: 638.
5. See also Meštrović and Brown, 1986.
6. Parsons, 1937: 421
7. Reichenbach, 1962: 280.
8. For example, Gouldner, 1970.
9. Parsons and Platt, 1973: 86–89.
10. Myrdal, 1944.
11. Gouldner, 1970: 257.
12. Parsons, 1937: 417.
13. Parsons, 1937: 428.
14. Pemberton, 1956: 247, 250, 253.
15. Parsons, 1951: 516; 1952.
16. Parsons, 1951: 516.
17. Parsons, 1937: 425.
18. Davis, 1951: 12.
19. Goode, 1951; Parsons, 1954; Schneider, 1970.
20. MacIntyre, 1970: xi.
21. Pemberton, 1956: 255.
22. Parsons, 1937: 420.
23. Parsons, 1937: 211.
24. For further elaboration, see B. Johnson, 1977.

## 2. SOCIOLOGY, CHRISTIANITY, AND HUMANITY

1. See Berger and Luckmann, 1966.
2. Wrong, 1961.
3. Turner, 1974: 84, see also 90–91.
4. Turner, 1974: 111.
5. Lichtman, 1970: 80.
6. See Heddendorf, 1972.
7. Lichtman, 1970: 81.
8. Fichter, 1972: 113; see Strauss, 1956: 204.
9. Turner, 1974: 180.

10. Lichtman, 1970: 91.
11. Fichter, 1972: 117.

## 3. THEOLOGY LESSONS FOR SOCIOLOGY

1. Gutiérrez, 1973: 9.
2. Baum, 1975; Küng, 1980.
3. An enlightened American Christian exception, however, is Mc-Govern, 1980.
4. For a discussion of the impact of sociology on Catholic theology, see Baum, 1979: 99–128.
5. This point should not be overstated, however. Clearly there have been a number of sociologists whose sociological work has been informed by their theological or humanistic values. Important examples include Robert Park, C. Wright Mills, Thomas O'Dea, Alvin Gouldner, Joseph Fichter, and Alfred McClung Lee, each of whose value commitment is clear in his sociological work.
6. See, e.g., the work of Neal (1977) or McAllister (1984).
7. Lyon, 1983: 227.
8. Wiles, 1976: 1.
9. Küng, 1980, 1984.
10. Richardson, 1969: 335.
11. Häring, 1981: 233.
12. Diener and Crandall, 1978.
13. Küng, 1980: 102.
14. Gouldner, 1962.
15. This is certainly still a minority view in the sociology of religion, not to mention sociology at large. Nor do all those who see it applaud it. According to Beckford (1985), for example, the taint of religion is one reason why the sociology of religion is isolated from the mainstream of sociological work. A recent article by Robbins (1983) speaks of a coming ferment within the sociology of religion. Many of the questions raised earlier about the value position of sociology in general, he argues, will be raised again in the sociology of religion precisely because they were not definitively answered previously. Answers are now more important than ever, for —as Robbins expresses it—"the beach is washing away."
16. Lundberg, 1961: 112.
17. Gouldner, 1962: 212.
18. In Martin et al., 1980: 2.
19. E. Becker, 1975; however, see Meštrović and Brown (1986) on the importance of rethinking *anomie* in these terms.

20. Richard Quinney's work on *Providence* (1980) provides at least one exception to the general trend.

21. Hollenbach, 1983.

## 4. THE SOCIOLOGICAL THEOLOGY OF H. RICHARD NIEBUHR

1. Niebuhr, 1928: vii.
2. See Niebuhr, 1960: 11, 21–38, 163–65.
3. Niebuhr, 1960: 65.
4. See Pfuetze, 1961: 3.
5. Niebuhr, 1945; 1963: 70–76; 1970: 105.
6. See Niebuhr, 1960: 72; Morris, 1963: ix-xxxv.
7. Niebuhr, 1960: 94–95.
8. Mead, 1963: 42–226.
9. See Niebuhr, 1960: 75, 152–55.
10. Niebuhr, 1960: 109, 121.
11. Niebuhr, 1960: 166–67.
12. Niebuhr, 1960: 152–53.
13. Mead, 1963: 75–82.
14. Mead, 1963: 150–51, 364–67.
15. Berger, 1963: 95.
16. See Mead, 1963: 362–67; 1967b: 610–11; Pfuetze, 1961: 87–89.
17. Niebuhr, 1960: 154.
18. Pfuetze, 1961: 82.
19. Mead, 1963: 136–37.
20. Mead, 1963: 186.
21. Mead, 1963: 200–203.
22. Mead, 1963: 214–22.
23. Mead, 1959: 14–19; 1967b: 486–89.
24. Niebuhr, 1960: 136–37; Mead, 1967a: 362–63; 1963: 221–22.
25. Niebuhr, 1960: 182–86.
26. Niebuhr, 1960: 58, 170, 179–81.
27. Niebuhr, 1960: 151, 183–87.
28. See, for example, Nottingham, 1971: 3; O'Dea, 1970: 202; Yinger, 1970: 2–3.
29. Scharf, 1970: 11.
30. See Swatos, 1984a.
31. James M. Gustafson is one of the very limited number who have productively entered Niebuhr's pattern of reasoning; see particularly his *Treasure in Earthen Vessels* (1961).

## 5. A SOCIOLOGICAL AND FRATERNAL PERSPECTIVE ON JAMES M. GUSTAFSON'S ETHICS

1. Particularly important was my attendance at "A Symposium: Assessments of James M. Gustafson's *Ethics from a Theocentric Perspective*" held at Washington and Lee University, Lexington, Virginia, September 26–28, 1985. I am grateful for both a typescript of the discussion at this event and Jim's comments and corrections on it and on earlier drafts of this essay.

2. In the course of preparing this essay, Jim reminded me that he wrote his University of Chicago/Chicago Theological Seminary B.D. thesis in 1951 on Weber (*Max Weber's Methodology*)—under James Luther Adams.

3. My interpretation of Weber is largely based upon the section "The Weberian Pattern" of Schluchter, 1981 (here, p. 160, schemes XXII): 18–60.

4. Schluchter, 1981: 49 (Weber's definition of theodicy).

5. Schluchter, 1981: 59.

6. Gustafson, 1985: 94.

7. Gustafson, 1981: 201–205.

8. From Jim's (corrected) reply to Paul Ramsey at the Symposium, Washington and Lee University, September 28, 1985.

9. Gustafson, 1981: chapter 4.

10. Gustafson, 1984: chapter 2.

11. Gustafson, 1984: chapter 3.

12. See Gustafson, 1981: 3–16, 115, 134, 136, 208, 211–25, 284ff.; 1984: 6–7, chapters 5–8.

13. Cohen, 1974: 23–31.

14. See Jim's reply to Paul Ramsey, quoted above.

15. Gustafson, 1984: chapters 2 and 3.

16. Gustafson, 1981: 103, 128, 149, 187, 315–16, 338–39; 1984: 4–22, chapter 9, 279–322.

17. Gustafson, 1981: 128–29.

18. Gustafson, 1981: 316.

19. Gustafson, 1984: 13.

20. Gustafson, 1984: 315.

21. Gustafson, 1981: chapter 7, 327–42; 1984: 32–33, 113, 302–19.

22. Gustafson, 1984: 338.

23. Gustafson, 1984: 317.

24. See Abramowski, 1982; Glassman and Murvar, 1984; Swatos, 1986.

25. Gustafson, 1981: 195, see also 129–36.

26. Gustafson, 1984: 306.

27. Gustafson, 1984: 317.
28. See M. Douglas and Tipton, 1983: especially Part I and 249–61.
29. Marianne Weber, 1975: 1–104.
30. John Milton, *Paradise Lost*, Book 4 (as quoted by Gustafson, 1984: 279).
31. Gustafson, 1984: 322.


## 6. ETHICS AND THE IMAGE OF THE SELF IN THE THEOLOGY OF STORY

1. Frei, 1974: 16.
2. Hauerwas, 1976: 344.
3. See Raines, 1973: 45.
4. Wrong, 1961; also see Dahrendorf, 1968; Fichter, 1972.
5. In line with this, the components included here are formal criteria which relate to a foundational anthropology. What is being tested is the *adequacy* of the image contained in the theology of story. It is not the intention of this essay to claim that the theology of story is in all respects more commendable than any other style, nor is it my intention to construct a theological doctrine of the self here; *however* the components selected do tend to suggest that *certain theological images are less than adequate.*
6. A relatively complete bibliography of the theology of story can be found in Stroup, 1975: 133–43. The various theologians of story do not agree on a single image of the self, but there are points of consensus in their work.
7. Crites, 1971: 297.
8. TeSelle, 1975: 1–2.
9. These points are more fully elaborated in D. Evans, 1963.
10. Other claims have been made for the significance of the theology of story; see Wiggins, 1975; Winquist, 1974; McClendon, 1974; Hauerwas, 1974.
11. McClendon, 1974: 36.
12. Several of these elements are mentioned by Gerhard von Rad in his commentary on this passage (Genesis 22: 1–19); see von Rad, 1971: 237–45.
13. Crites, 1971: 295.
14. Hauerwas, 1974: 20, see also 45, 71.
15. The ethicist of story has no interest (or certainly should have no interest) in excluding from view the role of principles in his or her focus on virtue and character. Stories that do not generate morally significant principles are no more sufficient to direct the moral life than are abstract ethical principles that are subject to perverse interpretation.

16. Estess, 1974: 426.
17. Estess, 1974: 432.
18. Wiggins, 1975: 20.
19. TeSelle, 1974: 634.
20. Hillman, 1967: 304.
21. Wiggins, 1975: 18.
22. Although the importance of internal meaning and the interior life has been recognized by theologians and ethicists, the full appreciation of that aspect of being has been eroded by the scientific worldview of the present. Crites indicates that this has happened through two strategies: *abstraction*, in which experience becomes non-narrative and atemporal (the basis of all science), and *contraction*, the constriction of attention to fragmented and disassociated immediacies. Both strategies threaten our ability to understand the coordinated flow of internal meaning. Crites (in Wiggins, 1975: 23–63), by contrast, does a superb job of remuddying the waters of experience. By erasing neat clarity and rejuvenating the possibility of transcendence, he restores theological ambiguity and experiential richness to their rightful place. In this way, the fullness of the internal life is given a reality *sui generis* which is reminiscent of Robert Bellah's argument for symbolic realism. The internal life is alive and well.
23. See Crites in Wiggins, 1975: 52–56.
24. Alfred Schutz's essay "On Multiple Realities" (1971: 207–59) is helpful in distinguishing symbolic meaning from external experience. The phenomenological approach appears eminently suited to the clarification of the relationship of experience and symbol.
25. Hauerwas, 1976: 341.
26. For a fascinating interpretation of the place of the story in psychoanalytic theory, see Hillman in Wiggins, 1975: 123–73.


# 7. ON FREEDOM, LOVE, AND COMMUNITY

1. Sorokin, 1937–41.
2. See Hillery, 1968, 1971.
3. See Hillery, 1982: 186–87.
4. See Hillery et al., 1977.
5. See 1 Corinthians 7: 4.
6. Nash, 1940: 148.
7. See Acts, chapters 2 and 4, for expressions of this communal ideal in early Christianity.
8. The corresponding Greek terms are *philia* and *storgé*; see Lewis, 1960.

9. "Therefore a man leaves his father and his mother and cleaves to his wife, and they become one flesh" (Genesis 2: 24).

10. Involvement is measured after Kanter, 1972; cohesion, Seashore, 1954. Partial gammas, controlling for age, group size, and education, do not alter the relationships, except that the gamma between involvement and group size is reduced somewhat (from $-0.489$ to $-0.255$); see Hillery, 1982: 199.

11. Boros, 1973:29

12. See Schmalenbach, 1961.

13. See Patterson, 1982.

14. See Hillery, 1982: 185–99.

15. These groups included the monasteries, two urban communes, a corps of women cadets, the staff of a boarding school for delinquent children, and a drug rehabilitation center. The last two groups had 73.3 and 16.7 percent believing in God, respectively.

16. Hillery et al., 1977.

17. See also Luther in Dewey and Gould, 1970. The popular Latin for Augustine's maxim is *Ama et fac quod vis*, while the original (in *Joann. 7: 8*) is *Dilige et quod vis fac*.

18. Goode, 1972; see also Warren, 1971.

19. This essay is a revised and abridged version of chapter 8, "Freedom, Love, and Community," in my book *A Research Odyssey*, a previous version of which appeared in *transaction/SOCIETY* 15/4 (May/June, 1978). Acknowledgment is given to several of the monks who have read and critiqued earlier versions, and especially to Father David Bock, O.C.S.O., of New Melleray Abbey, Father Casmir Bernas, O.C.S.O., of Holy Trinity Abbey, and Father Andrew Gries, O.C.S.O., of Holy Cross Abbey. Thanks also to Professor Roland L. Warren for helpful comments. Final responsibility for the way in which this assistance was used, of course, rests with the author.

## 8. THE POWER OF PRAYER: OBSERVATIONS AND POSSIBILITIES

1. E.g., Kolb, 1967.

2. There is no clear evidence that this is true: Must a chemist be an atheist or agnostic to do chemistry? With Gouldner—and Johnson and McAllister in this volume—I hold that much in this contention is mere ideology.

3. See Berger and Luckmann, 1963; and chapter 2 above. Gallup (1985: 45–46) shows that a fairly constant 90 percent of Americans pray—including "as many as three in four" of those who define themselves as

"unchurched." About 30 percent *pray twice a day or more*, while over half say grace "out loud" before family meals. *People pray!*

4. I am grateful to Tom Hood for several suggestions along the way in writing this paper.

5. Without wanting to generate unnecessary Freudian analyses, to be honest we must also recognize that prayer is also about impotence (on the part of supplicants).

6. This is not to say that prayer is *only* about power, but rather that power relationships are important to prayer, and prayer is a dimension of human power relationships.

7. It might be argued that in addition to Posthumous Power there should be a similar category regarding the interactions of various beings in the spirit world. On the contrary, however, prayers that ask one receiver/transmitter to affect another are practically without exception prayers that have a this-worldly terminus in their expectations.

8. This taxonomy is meant to exhaust the potential power relationships expressed in prayer. It is not, however, meant to imply that this is the only way to analyze prayer, but rather that there is an especial *sociological fruitfulness* in this style of analysis.

9. The legitimation of prayer is an important topic for further analysis. This has at least a two-way focus; i.e., legitimating prayer before the receiver/transmitter and legitimating prayer before fellow humans. In modernity at least, there are certain times at which prayer is considered appropriate, others at which it is inappropriate and then gray areas in which legitimations come most fully into play. As an example, I have copies of instructions from a public hospital for volunteer chaplains (community ministers), whose primary service is to visit religious "nones" and other patients who are reasonably prevented from obtaining the services of a clergyperson of choice. It is stated very explicitly in these instructions that the chaplain is *not* to pray with the patient unless requested to do so. Apparently it is legitimate for a *pastor* to pray based upon a self-definition of the situation, but not legitimate for prayer to be made if this role relationship has not been preestablished prior to the patient's admission to the hospital. Illness, then, does not automatically justify prayer; rather, *a social relationship justifies prayer.*

10. The phrase "methodological atheism" is Peter Berger's (1967). He credits it, in turn, to Anton Zijderveld. Pannenberg (in Peacocke, 1981: 4) astutely observes, however, "so-called methodological atheism ... is far from pure innocence." See Gaede (1981) and Whittaker (1981) for critique, commentary, and appreciation.

11. See, e.g., McGuire, 1982.

12. Festinger et al., 1964.

13. Bellah, 1967.
14. See Gallagher, 1981; Wallis et al., 1986.
15. Deutsch, 1953: 153–54 (emphasis added).
16. See Benson, 1984; D. Johnson et al., 1986.
17. On situationalism, see Swatos, 1984b.

## 9. THE INVISIBLE RELIGION OF CATHOLIC CHARISMATICS

1. Plato, *Republic* (597b).
2. Plato, *Cratylus* (390).
3. See J. Douglas, 1972: 28; McGuire, 1982: 19–20.
4. Robbins et al., 1973: 271.
5. See Glock and Stark, 1965.
6. See Rahner, 1966.
7. Câmara, 1971.
8. *Lumen Gentium*, article 8 (in Abbott, 1966: 23).
9. Dulles, 1978: 135.
10. See Miller, 1956: chapter 3.
11. Otto, 1958; Mauss, 1967; Durkheim, 1969; Eliade, 1957.
12. Otto, 1958: 45.
13. Joseph Cardinal Bernardin, speech at Fordham University, December 6, 1983.
14. See *Gaudium et Spes*, no. 59 (in Abbott, 1966: 265).
15. See Shiner, 1967.
16. See Bensman and Givant, 1986; Swatos, 1983, 1986.
17. Horkheimer, 1974; Marcuse, 1964.
18. Bellah, 1964: 371.
19. Luckmann, 1967.
20. See Fowler, 1981.
21. Tillich, 1957.

## 10. MILITANT RELIGION

1. Wuthnow, 1973.
2. Lewy, 1974: 483.
3. See Althusser, 1977.
4. R. Merton, 1968: 96–100.
5. This approach is illustrated by Glock and Stark, 1965.
6. See Weber, 1978: 212–54.
7. See Schoenfeld, 1987.
8. See C. Becker, 1959.

9. Hofstadter, 1966.

10. In Speer, 1984: 22.

11. Marx and Engels, 1976: 67–71.

12. Abercrombie et al., 1980; Parkin, 1979.

13. Marx and Engels, 1968: 96, 181.

14. Marx and Engels, 1975: 98.

15. G. Marx, 1967: 72.

16. Rokeach, 1970.

17. Marx and Engels, 1975: 62–64.

18. Cox, 1984: 144–45; see also Gutiérrez, 1973.

19. See Schoenfeld, 1974.

20. See the pastoral letter "Gospel and Revolution" by sixteen bishops of the Third World quoted in Lewy, 1974: viii (n. 7).

21. Rokeach, 1970.

22. See Lipset and Raab, 1978; Hofstadter, 1966.

23. In Cox, 1984: 29.

24. Rokeach, 1970.

25. In Chandler, 1984: 49.

26. Chandler, 1984: 46. Quoting again: "Christ was not a lamb, but a ram!"

## 11. THE PSYCHOLOGICAL CAPTIVITY OF EVANGELICALISM

1. Vitz, 1977: 70.

2. Vitz, 1977: 70–71.

3. Quebedeaux, 1974: 3–4.

4. Gallup, 1985: 38.

5. See Quebedeaux, 1978.

6. Witness, for example, the growth of Oral Roberts University as a serious academic enterprise.

7. Niebuhr, 1928.

8. Carnell, 1959: 113.

9. Bright, 1970: 196.

10. J. Evans, 1972: 769.

11. See Berger, 1963: 100–101.

12. See Berger, 1963: 36–37.

13. Allport, 1966.

14. See Moberg, 1986, on the controversy surrounding Anthony Campolo.

15. It seems irrelevant but appropriate to end as this paper has begun—

with a reference to the great (but not necessarily positive or correct) contribution of Freud to our contemporary way of thinking.

## 12. CLINICAL PASTORAL SOCIOLOGY

1. See Van Wagner, 1983.
2. See Lageman, 1984; Foegen, 1979.
3. See Weber, 1978: 243–45; 1117–20.
4. "Charismatic" here used in the classical Weberian sense, which has very little to do with the contemporary "charismatic movement."
5. See Kleinman, 1984.
6. See Hadden, 1969; Denison, 1985; Campbell, 1985.
7. Kelly, 1924; Thorton, 1970.
8. Thorton, 1970: 58.
9. See Asquith, 1982.
10. See Boisen, 1946.
11. Thorton, 1970: 62.
12. Greisman and Mayers, 1977: 61–62.
13. See Blasi, 1985: 23–40.
14. See Swatos, 1984b.
15. See Denison, 1985.
16. See Hughes, 1969.
17. Freidson, 1970.
18. Nisbet, 1962.
19. Schön, 1983: 130.
20. See, e.g., Peacock, 1971.
21. See Berger and Luckmann, 1966.
22. See Denison, 1985.
23. See Berger and Kellner, 1981.
24. Berger, 1979; also see Berger, 1969.
25. But see Quinney, 1980, 1982, 1986; Bailey, 1983.
26. See Cole, 1980: 123–41.

# Bibliography

The following abbreviations are used throughout the bibliography:

*ASR, American Sociological Review*
*JAAR, Journal of the American Academy of Religion*
*JSSR, Journal for the Scientific Study of Religion*
*RRR, Review of Religious Research*
*SA, Sociological Analysis*

Abbott, Walter M. (ed.). 1966. *The Documents of Vatican II.* Washington, D.C.: United States Catholic Conference.

Abercrombie, Nicholas, Stephen Hill, and Bryan S. Turner. 1980. *The Dominant Ideology Thesis.* London: Allen & Unwin.

Abramowski, Günter. 1982. "Meaningful life in a disenchanted world." *Journal of Religious Ethics* 10: 121–34.

Allport, Gordon W. 1966. "The religious context of prejudice." *JSSR* 5: 447–57.

Althusser, Louis. 1977. *For Marx.* London: Verso.

Anthony, Dick. 1982. "A phenomenological-structuralist approach to the scientific study of religion." *ReVision* 5: 50–66.

Anthony, Dick, and Thomas Robbins. 1975. "From symbolic realism to structuralism." *JSSR* 14: 403–14.

Anthony, Dick, Thomas Robbins, and Thomas E. Curtis. 1974. "Reply to Bellah." *JSSR* 13: 491–95.

Asquith, Glenn H. 1982. "Anton T. Boisen and the study of 'living human documents.' " *Journal of Presbyterian History* 60: 245–65.

Bailey, Edward I. 1983. "The implicit religion of contemporary society." *Religion* 13: 69–83.

Barth, Karl. 1961. *Church Dogmatics: III The Doctrine of Creation.* Edinburgh: Clark.

Baum, Gregory. 1975. *Religion and Alienation.* New York: Paulist Press.

_____. 1979. *The Social Imperative.* New York: Paulist Press.

Becker, Carl L. 1959. *The Heavenly City of the Eighteenth-Century Philosophers.* New Haven: Yale University Press.

Becker, Ernest. 1975. *Escape from Evil.* New York: Free Press.

Beckford, James. 1985. "The insulation and isolation of the sociology of religion." *SA* 46: 347–54.

Bell, Inge Powell. 1979. "Buddhist sociology." Pp. 53–66 in Scott G. McNall (ed.), *Theoretical Perspectives in Sociology.* New York: St. Martin's.

Bellah, Robert N. 1964. "Religious evolution." *ASR* 29: 358–74.

_____.1967. "Civil religion in America." *Daedalus* 96: 1–21.

_____. 1970. *Beyond Belief.* New York: Harper & Row.

_____. 1975. *The Broken Covenant.* New York: Seabury.

Bensman, Joseph, and Michael Givant. 1986. "Charisma and modernity." Pp. 27–56 in Ronald M. Glassman and William H. Swatos, Jr. (eds.), *Charisma, History, and Social Structure.* Westport, Conn: Greenwood.

Benson, Herbert. 1984. *Beyond the Relaxation Response.* New York: Time Books.

Berger, Peter L. 1963. *Invitation to Sociology.* Garden City, N.Y.: Doubleday.

_____. 1967. *The Sacred Canopy.* Garden City, N.Y.: Doubleday.

_____. 1969. *A Rumor of Angels.* Garden City, N.Y.: Doubleday.

_____. 1974. "Some second thoughts on substantive versus functional definitions of religion." *JSSR* 13: 125–33.

_____. 1979. *The Heretical Imperative.* Garden City, N.Y.: Doubleday.

Berger, Peter L., and Hansfried Kellner. 1981. *Sociology Reinterpreted.* Garden City, N.Y.: Doubleday.

Berger, Peter L., and Thomas Luckmann. 1963. "Sociology of religion and sociology of knowledge." *Sociology and Social Research* 47: 417–27.

_____. 1966. *The Social Construction of Reality.* Garden City, N.Y.: Doubleday.

Berger, Peter L., and Richard John Neuhaus. 1976. *Against the World for the World.* New York: Seabury.

Blasi, Anthony J. 1985. *A Phenomenological Transformation of the Social Scientific Study of Religion.* New York: Lang.

Boisen, Anton. 1946. *Problems in Religion and Life.* Nashville: Abingdon.

_____. 1960. *Out of the Depths.* New York: Harper & Row.

Boros, Ladislaus. 1973. *We Are Future*. Garden City, N.Y.: Doubleday.

Bright, Bill. 1970. *Come Help Change the World*. Old Tappan, N.J.: Revell.

Bromley, David G., and Anson D. Shupe, Jr. (eds.). 1984. *New Christian Politics*. Macon, Ga.: Mercer University Press.

Buber, Martin. 1958. *I and Thou*. New York: Scribners.

Câmara, Hélder. 1971. *Revolution through Peace*. New York: Harper & Row.

Campbell, Alastair V. 1985. *Professionalism and Pastoral Care*. Philadelphia: Fortress.

Campolo, Anthony. 1983. *A Reasonable Faith*. Waco, Texas: Word.

Carnell, Edward. 1959. *The Case for Orthodox Theology*. Philadelphia: Westminster.

Cavan, Ruth Shonle. 1983. "The Chicago school of sociology, 1918–1933." *Urban Life* 11: 407–20.

Cavanaugh, Michael A. 1982. "Pagan and Christian." *SA* 43: 109–30.

Chandler, Ralph Clark. 1984. "The wicked shall not bear rule." Pp. 41–62 in David G. Bromley and Anson D. Shupe, Jr. (eds.), *New Christian Politics*. Macon, Ga.: Mercer University Press.

Cohen, Abner. 1974. *Two Dimensional Man*. Berkeley: University of California Press.

Cole, Stephen M. 1980. *Sociological Method*. Boston: Houghton Mifflin.

Coste, René. 1985. *Marxist Analysis and Christian Faith*. Maryknoll, N.Y.: Orbis Books.

Cox, Harvey. 1984. *Religion in the Secular City*. New York: Simon and Schuster.

Crites, Stephen. 1971. "The narrative quality of experience." *JAAR* 39: 291–311.

Dahrendorf, Ralf. 1968. "Homo sociologicus." Pp. 19–87 in *Essays in the Theory of Society*. Stanford, Calif.: Stanford University Press.

Davis, Kingsley. 1951. "Introduction." Pp. 11–17 in William J. Goode, *Religion among the Primitives*. Glencoe, Ill.: Free Press.

Denison, Richard Eugene, Jr. 1985. "A charge to keep." Unpublished D. Min. dissertation, University of Chicago Divinity School.

DeSanto, Charles P., and Margaret Poloma (eds.). 1985. *Social Problems: Christian Perspectives*. Winston-Salem, N.C.: Hunter.

DeSanto, Charles P., Calvin Redekop, and William L. Smith-Hinds (eds.). 1980. *A Reader in Sociology: Christian Perspectives*. Scottdale, Penn.: Herald Press.

Desroche, Henri. 1973. *Jacob and the Angel*. Amherst: University of Massachusetts Press.

Deutsch, Karl. 1953. *Nationalism and Social Communication*. New York: Wiley.

Dewey, Robert E., and James A. Gould (eds.). 1970. *Freedom: Its History, Nature, and Varieties.* New York: Macmillan.

Diener, Edward, and Rick Crandall. 1978. *Ethics in Social and Behavioral Research.* Chicago: University of Chicago Press.

Douglas, Jack. 1972. *Research on Deviance.* New York: Random House.

Douglas, Mary, and Steven M. Tipton (eds.). 1983. *Religion and America.* Boston: Beacon Press.

Dulles, Avery. 1978. *Models of the Church.* Garden City, N.Y.: Doubleday.

Durkheim, Emile. 1969. *Elementary Forms of the Religious Life.* New York: Free Press.

Dynes, Russell R. 1974. "Sociology as a religious movement." *American Sociologist* 9: 169–76.

Eliade, Mircea. 1957. *The Sacred and the Profane.* New York: Harcourt Brace Jovanovich.

Ellul, Jacques. 1970. *Prayer and Modern Man.* New York: Seabury.

Estess, Ted L. 1974. "The inenarrable contraption." *JAAR* 42: 415–34.

Evans, Donald D. 1963. *The Logic of Self-Involvement.* London: Oxford University Press.

Evans, J. Claude. 1972. "The Jesus explosion in Dallas." *Christian Century* 89: 767–69.

Falwell, Jerry. 1980. *Listen, America!* Garden City, N.Y.: Doubleday.

Festinger, Leon, Henry W. Riecken, and Stanley Schacter. 1964. *When Prophecy Fails.* New York: Harper & Row.

Fichter, Joseph H. 1972. "The concept of man in social science." *JSSR* 11: 109–21.

Foegen, J. H. 1979. "Clergy as counselors." *Personnel* 56 (July/August): 70–78.

Fosdick, Harry Emerson. 1943. *On Being a Real Person.* New York: Harper & Row.

Fowler, James. 1981. *Stages of Faith.* San Francisco: Harper & Row.

Frei, Hans. 1974. *The Eclipse of Biblical Narrative.* New Haven: Yale University Press.

Freidson, Eliot. 1970. *Profession of Medicine.* New York: Dodd, Mead.

Friedrichs, Robert W. 1974. "Social research and theology: end of the detente?" *RRR* 15: 113–27.

Gaede, Stan D. 1981. Review of Peter L. Berger, *The Heretical Imperative. JSSR* 20: 181–85.

————. 1985. *Where Gods May Dwell.* Grand Rapids, Mich.: Zondervan.

Gallagher, Tom. 1981. "Religion, reaction, and revolt in Northern Ireland." *Journal of Church and State* 23: 423–44.

Gallup, George, Jr. 1985. *Religion in America* (Report 236). Princeton: The Gallup Report.

Garrett, William R. 1974. "Troublesome transcendence." *SA* 35: 167–80.

Gill, Robin. 1975. *The Social Context of Theology.* Oxford: Mowbrays.

———. 1977. *Theology and Social Structure.* Oxford: Mowbrays.

Glassman, Ronald M., and Vatro Murvar (eds.). 1984. *Max Weber's Political Sociology.* Westport, Conn.: Greenwood.

Glassman, Ronald M., and William H. Swatos, Jr. (eds.). 1986. *Charisma, History, and Social Structure.* Westport, Conn.: Greenwood.

Glock, Charles Y. 1972. "Images of 'god,' images of man, and the organization of social life." *JSSR* 11: 1–15.

———. 1976. "Consciousness among contemporary youth." Pp. 353–66 in Charles Y. Glock and Robert N. Bellah (eds.), *The New Religious Consciousness.* Berkeley: University of California Press.

Glock, Charles Y., and Rodney Stark. 1965. *Religion and Society in Tension.* Chicago: Rand McNally.

Goode, William J. 1951. *Religion among the Primitives.* Glencoe, Ill.: Free Press.

———. 1972. "The place of force in human society." *ASR* 37: 507–19.

Gouldner, Alvin W. 1962. "Anti-minotaur: the myth of a value-free sociology." *Social Problems* 9: 199–213.

———. 1970. *The Coming Crisis of Western Sociology.* New York: Basic Books.

Greeley, Andrew M. 1977. *The American Catholic.* New York: Basic Books.

Greisman, H. C., and Sharon S. Mayers. 1977. "The social construction of unreality." *Dialectical Anthropology* 2: 57–67.

Gross, Martin. 1978. *The Psychological Society.* New York: Random House.

Gunn, Giles B. 1979. *The Interpretation of Otherness.* New York: Oxford University Press.

Gustafson, James M. 1961. *Treasure in Earthen Vessels.* New York: Harper & Row.

———. 1981. *Ethics from a Theocentric Perspective: Theology and Ethics.* Chicago: University of Chicago Press.

———. 1984. *Ethics from a Theocentric Perspective: Ethics and Theology.* Chicago: University of Chicago Press.

———. 1985. "The sectarian temptation." *Catholic Theological Society of America Proceedings* 40: 83–94.

Gutiérrez, Gustavo. 1973. *A Theology of Liberation.* Maryknoll, N.Y.: Orbis Books.

Hadden, Jeffrey K. 1969. *The Gathering Storm in the Churches.* Garden City, N.Y.: Doubleday.

Hadden, Jeffrey K., and Anson Shupe (eds.). 1986. *Prophetic Religions and Politics.* New York: Random House.

Häring, Bernard. 1981. *Free and Faithful in Christ: Light unto the World.* New York: Crossroad.

Hauerwas, Stanley. 1974. *Vision and Virtue.* Notre Dame, Ind.: Fides.

————.1976. "Story and theology." *Religion in Life* 45: 339–50.

Heddendorf, Russell. 1972. "Some presuppositions of a Christian sociology." *Journal of the American Scientific Affiliation* 24: 110–17.

Hillery, George A., Jr. 1968. *Communal Organizations.* Chicago: University of Chicago Press.

————. 1971. "Freedom and social organization." *ASR* 36: 51–65.

————. 1982. *A Research Odyssey.* New Brunswick, N.J.: Transaction.

Hillery, George A., Jr., Charles J. Dudley, and Paula C. Morrow. 1977. "Toward a sociology of freedom." *Social Forces* 55: 685–700.

Hillman, James. 1967. "*Senex* and *puer*: an aspect of the historical and psychological present." *Eranos Jahrbuch* 36: 301–60.

Hofstadter, Richard. 1966. *Anti-Intellectualism in American Life.* New York: Vintage.

Hollenbach, David. 1983. *Nuclear Ethics.* New York: Paulist Press.

Horkheimer, Max. 1974. *The Eclipse of Reason.* New York: Seabury.

Hughes, Everett C. 1969. "Are clergy a profession?" Pp. 149–54 in Olga Craven, Alden Todd, and Jesse Ziegler (eds.), *Theological Education as Professional Education.* Dayton, Ohio: American Association of Theological Schools.

Husserl, Edmund. 1970. *The Crisis of European Sciences and Transcendental Phenomenology.* Evanston, Ill.: Northwestern University Press.

Johnson, Benton. 1977. "Sociological theory and religious truth." *SA* 38: 368–88.

Johnson, Daniel M., J. Sherwood Williams, and David G. Bromley. 1986. "Religion, health and healing." *SA* 47: 66–73.

Kanter, Rosabeth Moss. 1972. *Commitment and Community.* Cambridge, Mass.: Harvard University Press.

Kelley, Dean M. 1972. *Why Conservative Churches Are Growing.* New York: Harper & Row.

Kelly, Robert T. 1924. *Theological Education in America.* New York: Doran.

Kleinman, Sherryl. 1984. *Equals Before God.* Chicago: University of Chicago Press.

Kolb, William L. 1967. "Sociology and the Christian doctrine of man." Pp. 360–69 in Edward Cell (ed.), *Religion and Contemporary Western Culture.* Nashville: Abingdon.

Küng, Hans. 1980. *Does God Exist?* Garden City, N.Y.: Doubleday.

————. 1984. *Eternal Life.* Garden City, N.Y.: Doubleday.

Lageman, August G. 1984. "Marketing pastoral counseling." *Journal of Pastoral Care* 38: 274–80.

Lenski, Gerhard. 1961. *The Religious Factor*. Garden City, N.Y.: Doubleday.

Lewis, C. S. 1960. *The Four Loves*. New York: Harcourt, Brace.

Lewy, Guenther. 1974. *Religion and Revolution*. New York: Oxford University Press.

Lichtman, Richard. 1970. "Symbolic interactionism and social reality." *Berkeley Journal of Sociology* 15: 75–94.

Lipset, Seymour Martin, and Earl Raab. 1978. *The Politics of Unreason*. Chicago: University of Chicago Press.

Luckmann, Thomas. 1967. *The Invisible Religion*. New York: Macmillan.

Lundberg, George. 1961. *Can Science Save Us?* New York: Longmans, Green.

_____. 1964. *Foundations of Sociology*. New York: McKay.

Lyman, Stanford M. 1978. *The Seven Deadly Sins: Society and Evil*. New York: St. Martin's.

Lyon, David. 1976. *Christians & Sociology*. Downers Grove, Ill.: InterVarsity Press.

_____. 1983. "The idea of a Christian sociology." *SA* 44: 227–42.

MacIntyre, Alasdair. 1970. *Metaphysical Beliefs*. New York: Schocken.

Macquarrie, John. 1966. *Principles of Christian Theology*. New York: Scribners.

Marcuse, Herbert. 1964. *One-Dimensional Man*. Boston: Beacon.

Martin, David, John Orme Mills, and W.S.F. Pickering (eds.). 1980. *Sociology and Theology*. New York: St. Martin's.

Marx, Gary T. 1967. "Religion: opiate or inspiration of civil rights militancy among negroes?" *ASR* 32: 64–72.

Marx, Karl, and Friedrich Engels. 1968. *Selected Works*. Moscow: Progress Publishers.

_____. 1975. *On Religion*. Moscow: Progress Publishers.

_____. 1976. *The German Ideology*. Moscow: Progress Publishers.

Mauss, Marcel. 1967. *The Gift*. New York: Norton.

McAllister, Ronald J. 1984. "Toward a socio-theology of change." *New England Sociologist* 5: 113–23.

McClendon, James Wm., Jr. 1974. *Biography as Theology*. Nashville: Abingdon.

McGovern, Arthur F. 1980. *Marxism*. Maryknoll, N.Y.: Orbis Books.

McGuire, Meredith. 1982. *Pentecostal Catholics*. Philadelphia: Temple University Press.

Mead, George Herbert. 1959. *The Philosophy of the Present*. LaSalle, Ill.: Open Court.

————. 1963. *Mind, Self, and Society*. Chicago: University of Chicago Press.

————. 1967a. *Movements of Thought in the Nineteenth Century*. Chicago: University of Chicago Press.

————. 1967b. *Philosophy of the Act*. Chicago: University of Chicago Press.

Meagher, Robert E. 1978. *An Introduction to Augustine*. New York: NYU Press.

Merton, Robert K. 1968. *Social Theory and Social Structure*. New York: Free Press.

Merton, Thomas. 1953. *The Sign of Jonas*. New York: Harcourt, Brace.

————. 1975. *The Silent Life*. New York: Farrar, Straus & Giroux.

Meštrović, Stjepan G., and Hélène M. Brown. 1986. "Durkheim's concept of anomie as dereglement." *Social Problems* 33: 81–99.

Miller, Perry. 1956. *Errand into the Wilderness*. New York: Harper & Row.

Mills, C. Wright. 1943. "The professional ideology of social pathologists." *American Journal of Sociology* 49: 165–80.

Moberg, David O. 1972. *The Great Reversal*. Philadelphia: Lippincott.

————. 1986. "A new inquisition." *Newsletter of the Christian Sociological Society* 13(2): 8–9.

Morris, Charles W. 1963. "Introduction." Pp. ix-xxxv in George H. Mead, *Mind, Self, and Society*. Chicago: University of Chicago Press.

Moss, Tony (ed.). 1986. *In Search of Christianity*. London: Firethorn Press.

Mouw, Richard J. 1973. *Political Evangelism*. Grand Rapids, Mich.: Eerdmans.

Mueller, Gert H. 1980. "The dimensions of religiosity." *SA* 41: 1–24.

Myrdal, Gunnar. 1944. "A methodological note on facts and valuations in social science." Pp. 1034–64 in *An American Dilemma*. New York: Harper.

Nash, Ogden. 1940. *The Face Is Familiar*. Boston: Little, Brown.

National Conference of Catholic Bishops. 1983. *The Challenge of Peace*. Washington, D.C.: National Conference of Catholic Bishops, United States Catholic Conference.

Neal, Marie Augusta. 1977. *A Sociotheology of Letting Go*. New York: Paulist Press.

Niebuhr, H. Richard. 1928. *The Social Sources of Denominationalism*. New York: Holt.

————. 1945. "The ego-alter dialectic and the conscience." *Journal of Philosophy* 42: 352–59.

————. 1956. *Christ and Culture*. New York.. Harper & Row.

————. 1959. *The Kingdom of God in America*. New York: Harper & Row.

————. 1960. *The Meaning of Revelation*. New York: Macmillan.

————. 1963. *The Responsible Self*. New York: Harper & Row.

————. 1970. *Radical Monotheism and Western Culture*. New York: Harper & Row.

Nisbet, Robert. 1962. "Sociology as an art form." *Pacific Sociological Review* 14: 21–34.

Nottingham, Elizabeth K. 1971. *Religion: A Sociological View*. New York: Random House.

O'Dea, Thomas F. 1970. *Sociology and the Study of Religion*. New York: Basic Books.

Otto, Rudolf. 1958. *The Idea of the Holy*. New York: Oxford University Press.

Pannenburg, Wolfhart. 1976. *Theology and the Philosophy of Science*. Philadelphia: Westminster.

Parkin, Frank. 1979. *Marxism and Class Theory*. New York: Columbia University Press.

Parsons, Talcott. 1937. *The Structure of Social Action*. New York: Macmillan.

————. 1951. *The Social System*. Glencoe, Ill.: Free Press.

————. 1952. "Religious perspectives of college teaching: sociology and social psychology." Pp. 286–337 in Hoxie N. Fairchild (ed.), *Religious Perspectives of College Teaching*. New York: Ronald.

————. 1954. "The theoretical development of the sociology of religion." Pp. 197–211 in *Essays in Sociological Theory*. Glencoe, Ill.: Free Press.

Parsons, Talcott, and Gerald Platt. 1973. *The American University*. Cambridge, Mass.: Harvard University Press.

Patterson, Orlando. 1982. *Slavery and Social Death*. Cambridge, Mass.: Harvard University Press.

Peacock, James L. 1971. "The southern protestant ethic disease." Pp. 108–13 in J. Kenneth Morland (ed.), *The Not So Solid South*. Athens: University of Georgia Press.

Peacocke, A. R. (ed.). 1981. *The Sciences and Theology in the Twentieth-Century*. Notre Dame, Ind.: University of Notre Dame Press.

Pemberton, Prentiss L. 1956. "An examination of some criticisms of Talcott Parsons' sociology of religion." *Journal of Religion* 36: 241–56.

Pfuetze, Paul E. 1961. *Self, Society, Existence*. New York: Harper & Row.

Planas, Ricardo. 1986. *Liberation Theology*. Kansas City, Mo.: Sheed & Ward.

Poloma, Margaret M. 1982. "Toward a Christian sociological perspective." *SA* 43: 95–108.

Quebedeaux, Richard. 1974. *The Young Evangelicals*. New York: Harper & Row.

————. 1978. *The Worldly Evangelicals*. New York: Harper & Row.
Quinney, Richard. 1980. *Providence*. New York: Longman.
————. 1982. *Social Existence*. Beverly Hills, Calif.: Sage.
————. 1986. "A traveler on country roads." *Landscape* 29: 21–28.
Rahner, Karl. 1966. *The Church after the Council*. New York: Herder and Herder.
Raines, John C. 1973. "Theodicy and politics." *Worldview* 16(4): 44–48.
Raschke, Carl A. 1978. "The end of theology." *JAAR* 46: 159–79.
Reichenbach, Hans. 1962. *The Rise of Scientific Philosophy*. Berkeley: University of California Press.
Richardson, Alan. 1969. *A Dictionary of Christian Theology*. Philadelphia: Westminster.
Robbins, Thomas. 1983. "The beach is washing away." *SA* 44: 207–14.
Robbins, Thomas, Dick Anthony, and Thomas E. Curtis. 1973. "The limits of symbolic realism." *JSSR* 12: 259–71.
Rogers, Carl. 1963. *On Becoming a Person*. Boston: Houghton Mifflin.
Rokeach, Milton. 1970. "Religious values and social compassion." *RRR* 12: 24–39.
Ross, Edward Alsworth. 1973. *Sin and Society*. New York: Harper & Row.
Scharf, Betty R. 1970. *The Sociological Study of Religion*. New York: Harper & Row.
Schluchter, Wolfgang. 1981. *The Rise of Western Rationalism*. Berkeley: University of California.
Schmalenbach, Herman. 1961. "The sociological category of communion." Pp. 331–47 in Talcott Parsons (ed.), *Theories of Society*. New York: Free Press.
Schneider, Louis. 1970. *Sociological Approach to Religion*. New York: Wiley.
Schoenfeld, Eugen. 1974. "Love and justice, the effect of religious values on liberalism and conservatism." *RRR* 16: 41–46.
————. 1987. "Justice: the illusive concept in Christianity." *RRR* 28: (forthcoming).
Schön, Donald A. 1983. *The Reflective Practitioner*. New York: Basic Books.
Schumacher, E. F. 1973. *Small Is Beautiful*. New York: Harper & Row.
Schutz, Alfred. 1971. "On multiple realities." Pp. 207–59 in *Collected Papers* I. The Hague: Nijhoff.
Scott, Donald M. 1978. *From Office to Profession*. Philadelphia: University of Pennsylvania Press.
Seashore, Stanley E. 1954. *Group Cohesiveness in the Industrial Work Group*. Ann Arbor, Mich.: Survey Research Center, Institute for Social Research, University of Michigan.

Shiner, Larry. 1967. "The concept of secularization in empirical research." *JSSR* 6: 207–20.

Sider, Ronald J. 1977. *Rich Christians in an Age of Hunger*. Downers Grove, Ill.: InterVarsity Press.

Sorokin, Pitirim. 1937–41. *Social and Cultural Dynamics*. New York: American Book Company.

Speer, James A. 1984. "The new Christian right and its parent company." Pp. 19–40 in David G. Bromley and Anson D. Shupe, Jr., *New Christian Politics*. Macon, Ga.: Mercer University Press.

Stark, Rodney, and Charles Y. Glock. 1968. *American Piety*. Berkeley: University of California Press.

Strauss, Anselm. 1956. *The Social Psychology of George Herbert Mead*. Chicago: University of Chicago Press.

Stroup, George W. 1975. "A bibliographical critique." *Theology Today* 32: 133–43.

Swatos, William H., Jr. 1977. "The comparative method and the special vocation of the sociology of religion." *SA* 38: 106–14.

_____. 1980. "Liturgy and lebensform." *Perspectives in Religious Studies* 8: 38–49.

_____. 1983. "Enchantment and disenchantment in modernity." *SA* 44: 321–38.

_____. 1984a. *Faith of the Fathers*. Bristol, Ind.: Wyndham Hall.

_____. 1984b. "Religion, secularization, and social process." *New England Sociologist* 5: 95–112.

_____. 1986. "The disenchantment of charisma." Pp. 129–46 in Ronald M. Glassman and William H. Swatos, Jr. (eds.), *Charisma, History, and Social Structure*. Westport, Conn.: Greenwood.

TeSelle, Sallie. 1974. "Parable, metaphor, and theology." *JAAR* 42: 630–45.

_____. 1975. *Speaking in Parables*. Philadelphia: Fortress.

Thorton, Edward E. 1970. *Professional Education for the Ministry*. Nashville: Abingdon.

Tillich, Paul. 1957. *Dynamics of Faith*. New York: Harper & Row.

Turner, Jonathan. 1974. *The Structure of Sociological Theory*. Homewood, Ill.: Dorsey.

Van Wagner, Charles A. 1983. "The AAPC." *Journal of Pastoral Care* 37: 163–79.

Vidich, Arthur J., and Stanford M. Lyman. 1985. *American Sociology*. New Haven: Yale University Press.

Vitz, Paul. 1977. *Psychology as Religion*. Grand Rapids, Mich.: Eerdmans.

von Rad, Gerhard. 1971. *Genesis*. Philadelphia: Westminster.

Wallis, Roy, and Steve Bruce. 1986. *Sociological Theory, Religion and*

*Collective Action*. Belfast: Department of Social Studies, The Queen's University.

Wallis, Roy, Steve Bruce, and David Taylor. 1986. *"No Surrender!": Paisleyism and the Politics of Ethnic Identity in Northern Ireland*. Belfast: Department of Social Studies, The Queen's University.

Warren, Roland L. 1971. *Truth, Love and Social Change*. Chicago: Rand McNally.

Weber, Marianne. 1975. *Max Weber*. New York: Wiley.

Weber, Max. 1978. *Economy and Society*. Berkeley: University of California Press.

Whittaker, John H. 1981. "Neutrality in the study of religion." *Bulletin/CSR* 12: 129–31.

Wiggins, James B. (ed.). 1975. *Religion as Story*. New York: Harper & Row.

Wiles, Maurice. 1976. *What Is Theology?* London: Oxford University Press.

Winquist, Charles. 1974. "The act of storytelling and the self's homecoming." *JAAR* 42: 101–13.

Wittgenstein, Ludwig. 1958. *Philosophical Investigations*. New York: Macmillan.

Wrong, Dennis H. 1961. "The oversocialized conception of man." *ASR* 26: 183–93.

Wuthnow, Robert. 1973. "Religious commitment and conservatism." Pp. 117–32 in Charles Y. Glock (ed.), *Religion in Sociological Perspective*. Belmont, Calif.: Wadsworth.

Yinger, J. Milton. 1970. *The Scientific Study of Religion*. New York: Macmillan.

# Index

Absurd, sociology of, 19
Adams, James Luther, 169 n.2
Agapé, 94–96, 100, 133
Allport, Gordon, 150
Anthony, Dick, 116
Aquinas, Thomas, 34

Bailey, Edward, 163
Barth, Karl, 32, 71, 144
Baum, Gregory, 27, 167 n.4
Becker, Ernest, 37
Becker, Howard, 19
Beckford, James, 167 n.15
Behaviorism, 16–23
Bellah, Robert N., 109, 122, 171 n.22
Berger, Peter L., 19, 29, 32, 62, 148, 163, 165 n.11, 173 n.10
Bloesch, David, 145
Boisen, Anton, 155–56
Bonhoeffer, Dietrich, 32, 39, 144
Buber, Martin, 43–44, 47
Buddhist social science, 39, 165 n.1

Cabot, Richard, 155
Câmara, Hélder, 118
Campolo, Anthony, 165 n.2, 175 n.14 (ch.11)

Campus Crusade for Christ, 147–48
Christian sociology, 54, 151
Church-sect typology, 8, 119
Civil religion, 109, 111–12, 129
Clinical pastoral education (CPE), 153, 156
Cohen, Abner, 62
Comte, Auguste, 5, 28–29, 32
Conflict (social), 15–24
Coser, Lewis, 21
Creationism (doctrine of creation), 142
Crites, Stephen, 73–74, 76, 171 n.22

Davis, Kingsley, 10
Deutsch, Karl, 111
Dulles, Avery, 118–19
Durkheim, Emile, 5, 8, 16, 27, 62, 101–2, 120, 157

Eliade, Mircea, 120
Ellul, Jacques, 104
Engels, Friedrich, 130–31
Estess, Ted, 78
Ethic of conviction, 59–67
Ethic of responsibility, 38, 59–67

Ethics, 34–39, 57–83, 112, 128, 142
Ethnomethodology, 19
Evil, 16, 19, 24, 37, 142

Faith development (theory of), 122–23
Falwell, Jerry, 129, 134–35
Feuerbach, Ludwig, 32, 131
Fichter, Joseph H., 22, 24, 167 n.5
Fletcher, Joseph, 71
Fosdick, Harry Emerson, 143–44
Fowler, James, 122
Frei, Hans, 69
Freidson, Eliot, 158
Freud, Sigmund (Freudianism), 27, 32, 141, 173 n.5, 175 n.15 (ch. 11)
Friedrichs, Robert W., 3
Functionalism, 16–23, 125–26, 155, 158

Gallup, George (Gallup poll), 145, 172 n.3
Garfinkle, Harold, 19
Gill, Robin, 28
Goffman, Erving, 19
Goode, William J., 101
Gouldner, Alvin, 8, 34, 36, 167 n.5, 172 n.2
Gross, Martin, 146
Gustafson, James M., 57, 60–68, 168 n.31, 169 nn.1, 2
Gutiérrez, Gustavo, 27, 39, 131

Häring, Bernard, 34
Hauerwas, Stanley, 77, 82
Hegel, Georg Friedrich, 27, 32, 130
Hillman, James, 69, 80, 171 n.26
Horkheimer, Max, 121

Inductive theology, 163–64
"I-Thou," 43–44, 48

Kant, Immanuel, 15, 17, 20, 34, 39, 43, 120
Kelley, Dean, 144
Keynes, John M., 164
King, Martin Luther, Jr., 131
Kuhn, Thomas, 164
Küng, Hans, 27, 32, 35

Labeling theory, 19
Lee, Alfred McClung, 167 n.5
Liberation theology, 27, 33, 39, 55, 131–32
Lichtman, Richard, 21–23
Luckmann, Thomas, 19, 62, 122
Lundberg, George (*Can Science Save Us?*), 17, 36, 116
Lyman, Stanford, 19, 37
Lyon, David, 32

MacIntyre, Alasdair, 11
Marcuse, Herbert, 121, 157
Marx, Gary, 131
Marx, Karl, 5, 20–21, 27–28, 32, 39, 130–31, 155, 158
Marxism, 6, 8, 20–21, 23, 27, 125–26, 129–30, 155, 157
Mauss, Marcel, 120
Mead, George Herbert, 22, 42–53
Merton, Robert K., 18, 126
Mill, John Stuart, 132
Mills, C. Wright, 167 n.5
Mills, John Orme, 29, 36
Milton, John, 67
Moberg, David, 151
Monasteries, monastic life, 92–100, 104
Moore, Wilbert, 18
Mouw, Richard, 151
Mueller, Gert H., 165 n.12

Multidimensionality of religion
  ("5-D"), 8, 117, 126
Myrdal, Gunnar, 7

Niebuhr, H. Richard, 41–55, 145,
  168 n.31
Niebuhr, Reinhold, 72, 144
Nisbet, Robert, 159

O'Dea, Thomas, 167 n.5
Otto, Rudolf, 120
"Oversocialized" view of human
  beings, 18, 24, 72

Pareto, Vilfredo, 10–11
Park, Robert, 167 n.5
Parsons, Talcott, 5–12, 18
Pemberton, Prentiss, 9, 11
Phenomenology, 15–24, 82, 159,
  171 n.24
Plato, 115–16
Popper, Karl, 35
Positivism, 6, 15–24, 28, 32, 35,
  103
Prayer, 95–96, 103–13, 162–63

Quebedeaux, Richard, 144
Quinney, Richard, 163, 168 n.20
  (ch. 3)

Rahner, Karl, 32, 118
Revelation, 42–53
Robbins, Thomas, 116, 167 n.15
Rogers, Carl, 144
Rokeach, Milton, 131, 135
Role theory, 47–53
Ross, Edward Alsworth, 37

Schleiermacher, Friedrich, 120
Schluchter, Wolfgang, 58–60, 64
Schutz, Alfred, 171 n.24
Secularization (theory/thesis of),
  63, 66, 121, 155
Sider, Ronald, 151
Simmel, Georg, 20–21
Situational approach, situational-
  ism, 157–63
Situation ethics, 71, 161
Skinner, B. F., 17–18
Social gospel, 54, 135, 142, 146–
  47
Sorokin, Pitirim, 88
Spencer, Herbert, 5
Symbolic interactionism, 17–23

TeSelle, Sallie, 74, 79
Thielicke, Helmut, 71
Thomas, W. I., 157
Tillich, Paul, 32, 122, 144
Toennies, Ferdinand, 99, 119
Troeltsch, Ernst, 42, 119
Turner, Jonathan, 22

Value freedom, value neutrality
  (*wertfrei Soziologie*), 4–13, 29,
  30, 34–39, 112, 126

Weber, Max, 5, 7, 27, 29, 32, 38–
  39, 57–67, 93, 119, 121, 154,
  158, 161–62, 169 nn.2–4, 176
  n.4
Wiggans, James, 79–80
Wrong, Dennis H., 18, 24
Wuthnow, Robert, 125

Zijderveld, Anton, 173 n.10

# About the Contributors

*Jack O. Balswick* is Professor of Sociology and Family Studies at Fuller Theological Seminary in Pasadena, California. He is the author of several well-known articles and a popular book, *Why I Can't Say I Love You.*

*William R. Garrett* is Professor of Sociology at St. Michael's College, Winooski, Vermont. He has served as editor of *Sociological Analysis: A Journal in the Sociology of Religion* and as president of its sponsor, the Association for the Sociology of Religion. He is the author of numerous articles in the sociology of religion and two textbooks.

*Paul M. Gustafson* is Professor Emeritus of Sociology at Hiram College in Ohio. He has had a distinguished teaching career and has contributed to the sociology of religion both through service to professional organizations and articles and book reviews across several decades.

*Pierre Hegy* is a member of the sociology faculty at Adelphi University, Garden City, Long Island. He contributes papers regularly to professional society meetings and for several years has organized an extramural session on Christianity and Sociology at the American Sociological Association annual meetings.

*George A. Hillery, Jr.* is the co-founder and chair of the Christian Sociological Society and Professor of Sociology at Virginia Polytechnic Institute and State University. He has served as president of the Southern Sociological Society and is the author of two books: *Communal Organizations* and *A Research Odyssey.*

*Benton Johnson* is Professor of Sociology at the University of Oregon. The author of several seminal articles in the sociology of religion, he has served as president of both the Society for the Scientific Study of Religion and the Association for the Sociology of Religion. He has edited the *Journal for the Scientific Study of Religion* and written an introductory monograph to the work of Talcott Parsons.

*L. Shannon Jung* is a member of the religion faculty at Concordia College, Moorhead, Minnesota. He contributes regularly to journals in the field of social ethics and is author of an integrative religion-society-individual text, *Identity and Community.*

*Ronald J. McAllister* teaches sociology at Northeastern University, Boston. He contributes papers, articles, and book reviews to professional societies in the sociology of religion.

*Eugen Schoenfeld* was for many years chairman of the sociology department at Georgia State University, where he now is director of the interdisciplinary program in religious studies. A survivor of the Holocaust, he has lectured and written on the theme of religion and justice.

**About the Editor**

*William H. Swatos, Jr.* has taught at King College, Bristol, Tennessee, and more recently as a member of the sociology department of Northern Illinois University. He serves on the Board of Directors of the Religious Research Association and the Executive Board of the Association for the Sociology of Religion. He is the author of two monographs—*Into Denominationalism: The Anglican Metamorphosis* and *Faith of the Fathers: Science, Religion, and Reform in Early American Sociology.* With Ronald M. Glassman, he is editor of two other Greenwood Press books, *Charisma, History, and Social Structure* (1986) and *Bureaucracy Against Democracy and Socialism* (1987).